# Fill Your Cup

## The Exhausted Educator's Guide to Emotional Wellness

of viable resources, educators are left with little time to dedicate to themselves or their families, as all their spare time is devoted to providing what the school boards can't (or more likely won't) provide. It's a chronic situation and the best teachers are breaking down, many leaving the profession. So, what can they do? First, they have to care for themselves because, quite frankly, they're no good to anyone else until they can re-fill the empty cup.

Mike Veny's book, *Fill Your Cup: The Exhausted Educator's Guide to Emotional Wellness*, is a good starting point for refilling that empty cup. It's presented as a course, complete with questions, exercises, activities, resources, helpful links, and a useful suggested reading list. The first part of the book addresses the growing trend of mental illness and how teachers need to look after themselves and take care of their own mental health. Using a small-step approach, the book stresses teacher self-care, keeping teachers motivated and focused so they can do the job they always dreamed of doing: teaching. The second part addresses the growing issues of student mental health and how a teacher can help their students deal with their mental health. The book is well organized and can be read all at once or studied in small parts, following the suggested exercises and extra readings to further benefit a teacher's mental health. The bottom line is: teachers need to take care of themselves first before they can effectively and compassionately take care of their students.

—Emily-Jane Hills Orford

In the informative guide, *Fill Your Cup: The Exhausted Educator's Guide to Emotional Wellness* by Mike Veny, educators will find actionable tools for supporting their students and their own emotional well-being. According to the findings of a survey included in the work, 75% of the teachers reported experiencing job-related stress often compared to 40% of adults working in other fields. The techniques discussed help avoid burnout, manage stress, and guide readers on how to utilize time efficiently. The book explains that educators' emotional wellness is affected by their students' emotional well-being and by helping their students, teachers' emotional wellness improves. Through their interaction with students, educators can identify and assist students struggling with mental health issues. The book examines different strategies and approaches for improving emotional wellness and for tackling issues that may arise as educators support students.

*Fill Your Cup* by Mike Veny is a straightforward guide with easy-to-digest information relevant to the topic. It is well-organized in a step-by-step format that guides the educator in their emotional wellness journey and that of their students. The self-care techniques and the tools for avoiding and managing stress can be utilized by any teacher regardless of their environment or position. The techniques can also be employed by students and adults working in other areas. The work is fun and includes a Spotify playlist and a fitting track for each chapter. Useful, detailed activities that readers can use for improving and actualizing emotional wellness are added as well. Various mental health resources are included at the end of the book. The book is a timely guide with practical self-care tools that readers and educators will find helpful.

—Edith Wairimu

*Being an educator comes with its own types of stress and challenges. It can take quite a toll on one's mental health. Fill Your Cup is a self-help guidebook by certified Corporate Wellness Specialist and best-selling author on mental health Mike Veny. This book is aimed at helping educators deal with the pressures of their job by providing tools and exercises that can be used in their everyday lives. Mike Veny encourages educators to delegate aspects of their work, make time for themselves with efficient time management, practice self-care, and shows readers how to plan for the future. The latter half of the book deals with supporting student wellness, which includes cultivating a mentally healthy environment and knowing how to have a mental health conversation with one's students.*

*Mental health awareness is one of the most important considerations of workplace environments nowadays, and education is a sector where mental health wellness is all the more challenging because of a whole host of reasons. Author Mike Veny offers some practically applicable tools and valuable insights through Fill Your Cup to help educators navigate mental health issues and help their students do the same. At the end of each chapter, there are reflection questions to make readers engage and evaluate themselves in relation to the content of the respective chapter. The book is short and concise and written in an accessible style that is easy to navigate. Overall, I found Fill Your Cup very educational and informative and will recommend it to all educators out there.*

*—Pikasho Deka*

*Fill Your Cup: The Exhausted Educator's Guide to Emotional Wellness by Mike Veny is a must-have for educators. Mike Veny is on a mission to support educators and empower their personal and professional growth. As the pandemic added more pressure and stress to their profession, educators who are feeling burned out, unappreciated, depressed, anxious, or lost, can now use this practical guide to take better care of themselves and take control over their time. This book helps teachers feel more motivated and focused. It shows them how to maximize their impact on their students by offering some practical self-care solutions, real, proven techniques, exercises, and more. Every tool and resource presented in this book helps educators with their health and well-being.*

*Fill Your Cup by Mike Veny is a promising contribution to reducing teachers' intent-to-leave teaching. It's so precise, helpful, well-written, and easy to understand. I found myself highlighting many nuggets of wisdom while reading. This thoughtful guide is a valuable resource as it examines the eight dimensions of wellness, the importance of the coping ahead method, the myths that surround mental health, self-care activities for one's mental, physical, spiritual, and social well-being, and more. It's an essential read for all teachers as it shows them how to identify the students who are struggling with a mental health challenge, and how to advocate for them. I recommend this empowering guide to all educators who want to have their cup full personally and professionally to teach with more confidence and to influence their students' lives positively.*

*—Emma Megan*

*Fill Your Cup: The Exhausted Educator's Guide to Emotional Wellness is a motivational book by Mike Veny. The author outlines the reasons why educators experience increased stress and anxiety, and he outlines various ways in which educators can reawaken their desire and continue on their path in education. He offers some inspiration by relating his own experiences and helps readers find ways to manage stress while providing examples of ways in which educators may increase productivity happily and efficiently. Veny includes the wellness of students as he discusses the way educators can impact a student's life and suggests ways to address student mental health concerns while focusing on the individual's emotional well-being.*

*Fill Your Cup is a useful tool to start meaningful conversations about mental health and healthy boundaries. This book will certainly have an impact on anyone who reads it and applies the messages in their life! Mike Veny has been surrounded by educators during his career, and he's monitored the effect the profession has had on them. The author presents his points with clear statistics as he makes his case for self-care. I particularly enjoyed the songs that accompanied each chapter, providing a musical theme to each section. The most helpful part of the book is the extensive compilation of resources for teachers. It is quite a helpful, comprehensive list that covers an array of possibilities. This guide would make a wonderful addition to the bookshelf of any educator and it would be beneficial in a teacher's classroom.*

*—Courtnee Turner Hoyle*

*"Thanks to Mike's passion for helping others, our educators were able to take these strategies, replenish their cup, and renew their 'why'. The strategies, and connections that were built that day will continue to provide support and encouragement throughout the school year, but most importantly during stressful times."*

*—Angie Kovarik, Lexington Public Schools*

*"Attending to your emotional wellness is the most important focus you can have--your thoughts and mental health set the direction for every day and every single thing in your life.   Mike Veny's highly anticipated new book "Fill Your Cup: The Exhausted Educator's Guide to Emotional Wellness" helps educators build habits that can impact their daily lives and the lives of their students.  Absolutely essential reading for every educator working to get their groove back—it is filled with useful and meaningful tools to reignite even the most burnt-out of educators."*

*—Beth White/Laura Obermann former educators and K-12 Senior Sales Reps at American Program Bureau*

*"It is clear from this book that Mike understands the reality of life as a teacher. So often we hear the message "self-care" over and over from news or social media, as if taking one more bubble bath is going to help our stress. This book is so much more than another pithy suggestion to "do self care". It gives concrete action steps to make small but significant changes that have a positive impact*

*immediately. As a teacher it's against my nature to write on books, but this book is made to be written in! Each chapter has a structured space to reflect and plan, as well as a playlist to enjoy while doing it! There are lots of books out there about mental health, but this is one of the rare gems that will have a lasting impact on its readers. Teachers, buy one for yourself and another for your friend. Administrators should read it, and then give it out to their staff. If you are stressed and exhausted, if you collapse on the couch when you get home from school, if you have nothing left for your family and friends by the end of the day, this book is for you!*

*—Sadie Wilson, AWARE Grant Specialist, Office of Coordinated Student Support Services*

# THANK YOU FOR BUYING THIS BOOK!

To receive special offers, bonus content and info on new releases, visit us online at www.mikeveny.com.

## MIKE VENY, INC. QUANTITY SALES DISCOUNTS

Mike Veny, Inc. titles are available at significant quantity discounts when purchased in bulk for client gifts, sales promotions, and premiums. Special editions, including books with corporate logos, customized covers, and letters from the company or its leader printed in the front matter, as well as excerpts of existing books, can also be created in large quantities for special needs.

For details and discount information for print and formats, contact team@mikeveny.com.

## WE'D LOVE TO HEAR YOUR FEEDBACK!

Fill Your Cup: The Exhausted Educator's Guide to Emotional Wellness can be purchased for educational, business, or sales promotional use. For information, please write:

Mike Veny
PO Box 2318
Monroe, New York 10949
USA

Published by Mike Veny, Inc.
First edition.
ISBN: 979-8-9850878-6-4

Cover design by Streetlight Graphics (www.streetlightgraphics.com)
Formatting by Streetlight Graphics (www.streetlightgraphics.com)
Directional Editing by Michael Luchies (www.michaelluchies.com)
Copy Editing by Laura Kaiser (www.wordhaveneditorial.com)
Proofreading by Christie Stratos, Proof Positive (www.proofpositivepro.com)

Fill Your Cup: The Exhausted Educator's Guide to Emotional Wellness® is a registered trademark of Mike Veny, Inc.
www.mikeveny.com

Contact Mike Veny at +1 (213) 458-8369 or by email at mike@mikeveny.com.

Learn more about Mike's most popular offerings:

www.mikeveny.com

# MORE BOOKS BY MIKE VENY

*Transforming Stigma: How to Become a Mental Wellness Superhero*
(Mike Veny, Inc. 2018)

*Transforming Stigma Workbook: How to Become a Mental Wellness Superhero*
(Mike Veny, Inc. 2019)

*Connectivity & Conversations: A Workplace Mental Health Course*
(Mike Veny, Inc. 2021)

*The ROI of Mental Wellness in the Workplace: Why It's
Necessary to Boost Employee Productivity*
(Mike Veny, Inc. 2022)

*How to Foster a Workplace Culture That Values Mental Wellness:
For Leaders and Managers Who Want Results*
(Mike Veny, Inc. 2022)

*Strategies for Discussing Mental Health with an Employee: Peace of Mind for Both of You*
(Mike Veny, Inc. 2022)

*How to Know When an Employee is Struggling: Easy Ways
to Understand Mental Health Concerns*
(Mike Veny, Inc. 2022)

*Talking About Mental Health at Work: Gain Confidence Around These Critical Conversations*
(Mike Veny, Inc. 2022)

All of the above are available at your local bookstore or may
be ordered by visiting www.mikeveny.com.

# CONTINUING EDUCATION CREDITS
**2 hours, 54 minutes** | 0.3 IACET CEUs

To receive credit for this, you must at least score 70% on the quiz. Only the first attempt at each quiz will be accepted. Many people find it helpful to print the quiz and keep it next to them when reading through the self-study guide.

**IMPORTANT:** To access the quiz, send an email to <u>team@mikeveny.com</u> with the following information:

- Your first name and last name

- Your best email address

- A copy of your receipt as proof of purchase. **A proof of purchase is required to get access to the quiz.**

Mike Veny, Inc. is accredited by the International Association for Continuing Education and Training (IACET). Mike Veny, Inc. complies with the ANSI/IACET Standard, which is recognized internationally as a standard of excellence in instructional practices. As a result of this accreditation, Mike Veny, Inc. is accredited to issue the IACET CEU.

Mike Veny, Inc. is also recognized by the Society for Human Resources Management (SHRM) to offer Professional Development Credits (PDCs) for SHRM-CP® or SHRM-SCP®. The company is also a Human Resources Certification Institute (HRCI) Accredited Provider.

Educators can use IACET CEUs for professional development in many states.

**We encourage you to check with your specific regulatory boards or other agencies to confirm that presentations from IACET Accredited Providers and presentations attended for IACET CEUs will be accepted by that entity.**

IACET CEUs are currently accepted for educators in:

| | | |
|---|---|---|
| Alaska | Massachusetts | New Hampshire |
| Arizona | Michigan | South Carolina |
| Georgia | Nebraska | South Dakota |

**NOTE to Michigan Educators**
Share your Certificate of Completion with your State Continuing Education Clock Hours (SCECHs) sponsor. Upon receiving it, they will convert the IACET hours and upload the SCECHs to your professional account for license renewal for you.

# OVERVIEW

This course will provide educators with tools and strategies for protecting and promoting their emotional wellness while supporting the well-being of their students.

# DESCRIPTION

You've heard the saying: *You cannot pour from an empty cup.*

As an educator, your cup may be empty, or close to it. After pouring yourself into your job and your students, there is often little left in that cup for you, your family, and for others. It may have led you to question your career choice and possibly even your true passion and purpose in life.

Filling your cup can be challenging, but it *can* be done. This course will give you the tools to fill your cup and restore your hope in being an educator. It will share real, proven techniques and exercises that are customizable for YOU.

# LEARNING OBJECTIVES

Upon completion of this self-study course, you will be able to:

- Spend your time and energy efficiently, productively, and peacefully

- Manage stress and prevent burnout

- Support students' emotional wellness, including having conversations about mental health

# DEDICATION

*This book is dedicated to Kayleen Holt.*

*Thank you for bringing your standard of excellence to the team at Mike Veny, Inc.*

*Thank you for challenging us to be more effective in executing our company mission.*

*Thank you for creating transformational learning experiences for the people we serve.*

## LISTEN TO THE MUSIC

This book is accompanied by a Spotify playlist and each chapter has a corresponding track. Scan this QR code to get the Spotify playlist made by Mike Veny.

# DISCLAIMER

**Trigger Warning:** This book discusses violence, self-harm, and suicide. If you or someone you know may be struggling with suicidal thoughts, you can call the **U.S. National Suicide Prevention Lifeline at 800-273-TALK (8255)** any time day or night.

**Disclaimer:** The purpose of this book is to educate. The author and/or publisher shall have neither liability nor responsibility to anyone with respect to any loss or damage caused, directly or indirectly, by the information contained in this book. The author is not a mental health professional. If you need medical help, please consult a doctor. **If you are in an emergency, please call 911.**

**Affiliate Links:** This book may contain affiliate links, which means the author and/or publisher may receive a commission if you make a purchase using these links.

**Limit of Liability/Disclaimer of Warranty:** While the publisher and author have used their best efforts in preparing this book, they make no representations or warranties with respect to the accuracy or completeness of the contents of this book and specifically disclaim any implied warranties of merchantability or fitness for a particular purpose. No warranty may be created or extended by sales representatives or written sales materials. The advice and strategies contained herein may not be suitable for your situation. You should consult with a professional where appropriate. Neither the publisher nor the author shall be liable for damages arising herefrom.

**Author Note:** Throughout this book the author uses the terms "mental health challenges", "mental health concerns" and "mental health conditions" in places where one might typically say "mental health issues" or "mental illness". He made the decision to do this because it feels less stigmatizing to him.

Some names and identifying details have been changed to protect the privacy of individuals.

We hope you find this book to be useful. If you have any feedback or questions, here's how to contact the author:

Mike Veny
Mobile: +1 (213) 458-8369
Email: mike@mikeveny.com
www.mikeveny.com

# TABLE OF CONTENTS

# HOW TO USE THIS BOOK

"You can't pour from an empty cup. Take care of yourself first."

— *Author Unknown*

This quote expresses the philosophy on which this book is based. You know that self-care is important and you're ready to invest in yourself.

Think of this book as a guide.

**This book is meant to be short and sweet.**

You're busy and you want answers now. I hope to give you some practical self-care solutions that you can apply immediately.

**This book is meant to be educational.**

If you read this book, you will learn how to take better care of yourself. I share resources, tools and tips that have been thoroughly vetted by educators and the team at Mike Veny, Inc.

**This book is meant to be a resource to reference in the future.**

The appendices alone make owning this book worth it, trust me. There's a lot here for you.

## DIFFERENT WAYS TO USE THIS BOOK

There are many different ways this book could be used. Here are some suggestions:

1. Read it straight through.

2. Allow your written responses or conversations in a group discussion to go whatever direction they choose. Use the space provided for your responses or use your favorite journal.

3. Start anywhere in the book. Although the sections and questions are structured in a way that I feel will be the most beneficial, do not feel bound to go in order.

4. Read a specific chapter or section that is useful to you, and come back later to other sections or chapters as you need them.

5. If you are using this book to guide you in your journaling, free yourself from distractions

and complete sections of the workbook in a space you're comfortable in. Consider putting your phone on silent, closing out your email inbox, and putting on some calming music.

6. Schedule more time than you think is needed to complete each section.

## HOW I USE THIS BOOK IN KEYNOTES & WORKSHOPS

When I deliver live and virtual keynotes, workshops, and professional development for educators, I often encourage attendees to get this book.

**But Do It Your Own Way**

There's no "right" or "wrong" way to use this book, simply do what feels best to you and what works for you right now and come back to read the book again later. The content in this book is here to serve you in whatever way you need.

# INTRODUCTION

Whom a cup is empty, what do you do with it?

You wash it, throw it away, or you fill it back up.

As an educator, your cup may be empty, or close to it. After pouring yourself into your job and your students, there is often little left in that cup for you, your family, and for others. It may have led you to question your career choice and possibly even your true passion and purpose in life.

There is good news and bad news about having an empty cup. Let's start with the bad news. The bad news is that only you can fill your cup, and filling your cup is challenging. There are no breathing exercises or stretches that can immediately refill a bare cup. The good news is that your cup doesn't need to be thrown away; it can be refilled, and you can benefit from the help of others when filling it.

An empty cup can cause a lot of things, from stress to depression. Educators are prone to having empty cups and are nearly three times as likely to experience depression according to a RAND survey funded by the National Education Association and American Federation of Teachers. Twenty-seven percent of public-school teachers surveyed reported symptoms of depression, compared to just 10 percent of all working adults, and more than 75 percent of teachers surveyed reported frequent job-related stress, which is nearly double the 40 percent of workers in other fields. Simply put, mental wellness is a serious issue for educators.

My name is Mike Veny, and I am on a mission to support educators like you in discovering the gift of emotional wellness. I want to help you fill your cup through unique learning experiences designed to empower your personal and professional growth.

In this book, I will give you the tools to fill your cup and restore your hope in being an educator. You will be able to use these today, tomorrow, next week, next month, and in years to come. This book will share real, proven techniques and exercises cultivated over the years, and each is customizable for YOU. This book contains a compilation of small steps that will keep you motivated and focused, and help you stay well while building our future by teaching and guiding our children. In Part 2 we will also talk about ways you can help students with their mental wellness, because when students' cups are full they can reach their potential and your classroom will be a happier place.

**CAUTION:** Before you continue, I must warn you.

While I teach people and have worked hand in hand with educators across the country for professional development and mental wellness, I am not an educator. I do not have a degree in education, and I do not have decades of experience teaching in a classroom. You know far better than I how difficult it is to be an educator; however, I have been surrounded by and have loved educators my entire life.

My team and family are full of current and former educators. My father was a teacher, Mother worked at a university, uncle was a superintendent (who expelled me from his school in the fourth grade), my cousin works in the field, and I have very close friends who are also educators. I also have spent much of the past decade talking, and most importantly, listening to educators.

I don't know firsthand what it's like to be in the classroom day after day with few resources and support, but what I know better than most is what it's like to have an empty cup, and I've spent decades desperately searching for ways to fill it. I have also dedicated myself to discovering and sharing how to fill the cups of others. I live with major depressive disorder, anxiety, and obsessive-compulsive disorder, also known as OCD. I was hospitalized in a mental health facility three times as a kid, was expelled from three schools, attempted to die by suicide at age ten, was violent at home, engaged in self-harm, and was on many medications.

I wrote *Transforming Stigma: How to Become A Mental Wellness Superhero* to tell my story and empower others to become what I have strived to be over the last decade—a mental wellness superhero. I am a Certified Corporate Wellness Specialist®, best-selling author on mental health, and one of the 100 most influential people in the healthcare industry according to PM360 ELITE (2017).

I have been able to limit the impact my mental health challenges have on my professional and personal life, and rise up to the challenge of helping others. Most importantly, I've been able to find happiness in what I do for a living. Through this happiness, I have been able to positively impact tens of thousands of lives. I want nothing more than for you to find that happiness and rediscover your love for being an educator. By completing the exercises in this book and incorporating techniques and practices into your routine, you will fill your cup. And this full cup will spill over to your peers, students, and family.

I have been working with hundreds of leading companies, teachers, and schools to improve the mental health and wellness of individuals, schools, and workplaces, including Merck, T-Mobile, Microsoft, CVS Health, Heineken, Ford, Wounded Warrior Project, and more. One of my favorite efforts I've completed with my company is Transforming Stigma® in the Classroom, a course that shows educators how to cultivate mental wellness for both students and teachers in the classroom.

*"You made a real impact on the lives of so many educators."*
— *Karen Barnes, Texas Region 10 Education Service Center*

*". . . he was the best speaker that we have brought to our district. We are definitely looking to bring him back to speak to our students/parents."*
— *Tiffany Owen, Horseheads School District*

*"With humor, optimism, and quality interventions, he provided us with useful strategies to employ in our classrooms."*
— *Cheryl Rosenfeld, Westcop Therapeutic Nursery and Head Start*

Books on mental wellness and self-care have a habit of diving deep into the why and barely touching on the how. My promise to you is that in this book, we will focus almost exclusively on the how. You are far too busy to consume hundreds of pages of content on research that unwinds the difficulties of being a teacher and states the full effect on your mental health; you experience this firsthand daily. I can promise you that when you implement these strategies into your life and routine, they will help prevent burnout and your cup will begin to fill.

Every week, I hear stories about teachers leaving the profession they once loved. Schools are desperately seeking to retain and recruit teachers and constantly seeking out substitutes. Because of this issue, education seems to be spiraling downward. There is a shortage of educators, and this has a direct impact on students and the teachers still in the classroom.

Few people start a career they intend to quit. Think about your own career. Did you spend the better part of a decade learning to master a profession that you planned to leave? But things change, and your cup starts to leak over time. Leaky cups can't support students.

Students trust their school to give them the basic skills they need to be successful in life. They gain these skills from their teachers, not just from lesson plans or by studying at home. They rely on interactions with educators. As an educator, you can maximize your impact by making every interaction with your student count.

*Do you feel that you are able to do that? Can you make the most of every interaction with your students, or are you feeling unable to give your students 100 percent because your cup is at 10 percent?*

If you believe you deserve to have a full cup (YOU DO!), then it's time to work on that. We will fill your cup with the following topics:

- Rediscovering your why
- Letting go of worry
- How to make the most of your time
- What it means to be well

- How to "cope ahead"
- Practicing self-care
- How to help students who are struggling

With a full cup, you will be able to give yourself, your students, and others in your life your very best. You will know why you became a teacher and why you are still teaching, and you will have the hope and tools you need to carry on with strength and purpose.

Thank you for your willingness to take this journey with me. Now let's fill that cup!

# PART 1: YOU

# CHAPTER 1: EMPOWERING YOURSELF AND YOUR STUDENTS WITH YOUR WHY

*"The person without a purpose is like a ship without a rudder."*

*– Thomas Carlyle*

**Artist:** Harold Melvin & the Blue Notes
**Album:** Wake Up Everybody - 1971
**Song:** "Wake Up Everybody"

Y OU BECAME AN EDUCATOR FOR a reason. That reason is your "why." Do you remember what your why was?

For most educators I speak with, the answer is no. As time passes, your why gets buried. It's now hidden under years' worth of worries and stress from feeling underappreciated to being underpaid, feeling burned out from the countless difficulties that come with your career choice.

In his book, Find Your Why, Simon Sinek wrote: "Fulfillment is a right and not a privilege. Every single one of us is entitled to feel fulfilled by the work we do, to wake up feeling inspired to go to work, to feel safe when we're there, and to return home with a sense that we contributed to something larger than ourselves."

Do you feel this way?

When you wake up, are you inspired?

When you're in front of your class, do you feel safe?

When you complete your workday, do you feel like you have contributed something of value to the world?

Since you are reading this book, I'm going to assume that your answer is no to at least one of the four questions above. Exhausted educators rarely feel fulfilled, inspired, safe, and of value. If you're feeling none of those things, that's okay. Feeling burned out, unappreciated, or lost doesn't mean you're broken, in the wrong career, or doing something wrong. It simply means you have a need—emotional wellness. In this book, I want to empower you to remember and utilize your why, and guide you toward feeling inspired and fulfilled, which will also have a lasting impact on your students.

Before diving into your why, I want you to take a minute to check in with yourself. After reading this sentence, put this book down, take three deep breaths, ask yourself the following question out loud, "How am I feeling about my life as an educator?", and answer it honestly out loud.

No seriously, do that. Right now!

Did you get through your response without swearing? Whether you did or you didn't, congratulations. Checking in on yourself and being honest about how you feel is a great first step toward supporting your emotional wellness and filling your cup. You might have said that you're worried, anxious, mad, sad, checked out—or even that you are thinking of making a career change. All of these feelings are common and reasonable. I encourage you to regularly check in with yourself. Ask, "How am I feeling about my life as an educator?" and answer it honestly. After answering each time, turn to your why.

So what was your why for becoming a teacher?

Your why is not just the reason you tell everyone you became a teacher when they ask. Simply liking children or having a parent who was also a teacher only scratches the surface. Your why includes the skills, passion, thoughts, and feelings you had when you decided to become an educator. What was it, specifically, about teaching that gave you a spark, that made you feel like you were pursuing what you were put on this Earth to do? What told you that this was what you had to do with your life? Or maybe the reason you first became a teacher was more practical than that: summers off, plenty of employment opportunities, benefits. In that case, ask yourself what difference can you make through your work? What will be your legacy?

Whether you remember it or not, every educator has a why; you just might have to rediscover it. When prompted below, shut off your phone, close your door, and find a quiet place. Take a minute or two to rediscover your why. Think back to when you decided to be an educator. Think about where you were living, what other career paths you were considering, the difference you wanted to make in the world, and what led you to finally choose to become an educator.

Take out a pen and a piece of paper, and write down your why, which is the reason you became an educator. Be as specific as possible while trying to keep it to one paragraph.

Go!

Now that you have your why, take three additional steps:

1. Make your why as concise as possible so it's easy to remember. If possible, trim it to one sentence.

2. Post a copy of your why somewhere you can see it daily (mirror, refrigerator, nightstand, car dashboard, etc.). This will allow you to remember why you do what you do.

3. Share your why with at least one person. You can post on social media, text a member of your family or a friend.

In regard to step three, this is where things may get difficult. Your why is personal, and sharing it may feel uncomfortable. This is a step that even I struggle with for two reasons:

1. Although there is a specific why that led me to become a drummer, entrepreneur, and then a mental health speaker, my why is ever-changing. My why as I write this book will likely change once or twice before this book is published.

2. My why is deeply personal. It's the foundation for everything I do in life, and it's not something I openly share with the world. I only share it with people I have a connection with on some level.

If you feel comfortable sharing your why with me, I would be happy to share my current why with you. Email me at mike@mikeveny.com.

My current why is written on an index card that I keep in my wallet. When I am feeling anxious, burned out, or like I want to give up, I take out my why, read it, and reflect on it. If I still believe in my why, I gain strength from reading it and am usually re-energized. If I question my why and am unsure that it is still a strong enough reason to continue down my current path, I know it warrants time for deep reflection. The changes you will make to your statement will likely be just small shifts once you know and are confident about your why.

Think of your why as the roots of an oak tree. What grows from this why is a trunk that serves as the core of your efforts, and several, or many, branches that grow from the trunk. For example, my why is not to write books, and not even solely to help teachers. My current why is centered around helping people with their mental health, and this book has developed as one of the branches on my why tree.

Several years ago, I published *Transforming Stigma: How to Become a Mental Wellness Superhero* with the why of helping a single person, and potentially, saving a life. If you are in need of immediate help, I encourage you to call the Suicide Hotline, which is free and confidential, at 800-273-8255. For this book, my why is to give educators real, simple, proven, and practical tools for navigating the most common problems that make your life and career difficult.

Educators aren't receiving the help they need, and this became clear to me even before the pandemic added pressure, stress, and difficult hurdles to the profession. This is especially true for women and Black teachers. Some educators are even leaving the profession. The pandemic exposed issues that were already hiding under the surface. I am not an educator, but I do work inside schools and have talked to thousands of educators and administrators. I've seen the challenges you face. Since the pandemic began, you have been asked to fit more and more into your already overloaded schedules.

In many conversations with educators, I've heard the same statements over and over, from "I'm overwhelmed" to "I just want to give up." It's why I decided to write this book. Everything I'm about to share with you has been vetted by classroom educators like you. We're going to focus not only on self-care, but also on specific strategies that can help you get more control over your time.

I know you may be thinking, "Mike, I've got too much to do and not enough time. Self-care is not going to fix this." I get it. Talking about self-care when you don't have time for self-care can feel inauthentic and like "lip service." I promise you that the tips and strategies I'll share will be useful to you and will help you be more emotionally well, and I sincerely thank you for taking a little time for yourself to improve your mental well-being, and so does your future self. When you are well, you have a better opportunity to teach your students effectively and have a profound impact on their lives.

In fact, *teachers saved my life.*

Before we go any further, let me tell you about some teachers who made a huge difference in my life. First, you need to know what I was like as a child. In my younger years, I had what you call behavioral problems. I was angry all the time, and I acted out violently. I didn't have a name for what I was feeling at the time, but I know now that I was struggling with depression and anxiety. But to my teachers, it just looked like I was a problem child. I was that kid. The one teachers hope they don't get in their classroom.

I was hospitalized for mental health challenges for the first time at age nine. I attempted to die by suicide at age ten. By the end of tenth grade, I'd been hospitalized three times, I was self-harming, and I had just been expelled from my third school.

Through all this time, the one thing that would calm me down, the one thing that made me feel really happy, was playing the drums. Somehow, my mother managed to get me an audition at the Long Island High School for the Arts—a performing arts high school—and I was accepted. When I was struggling and teachers noticed, they wouldn't scold me or send me to detention; they gave me a pass to leave class and play drums until I was ready to return to class. This was the best type of therapy I could possibly receive, and I truly believe it saved my life.

The teachers at that school responded to me with empathy. Unlike previous teachers, who relied on discipline alone—which just made me angrier—those teachers allowed me to productively work through managing my feelings. Not only did this therapeutic activity help me in the moment, my grades went up, and with the help of my psychiatrist, my medications went down. No more acting out. No more hospitalizations. No more self-harming, and no more attempts to die by suicide. I could write a whole book about the impact drumming has on people. Between the coordination and all the different areas of the brain working together, drumming is scientifically proven to go beyond just being a release. My last two years of high school were life-changing for me, and I started to see a future for myself—one where I could actually be happy.

While I don't know if these teachers were in touch with their why, it was clear that they had a larger goal for their students than simply having them learn the lesson of the day. They supported their students and adjusted to accommodate their needs. This shift, flexibility, and understanding is something I have thought of nearly every day since leaving that school.

This is the difference that you, as a teacher, can make. And by keeping your purpose top of mind each day, you can make a significant impact in the lives of countless students while supporting your own health and well-being.

## ACTIVITY 1.1: REFLECTION QUESTION

Why did you become an educator?

_____

_____

_____

_____

Where will you keep your why?

_____

_____

_____

_____

# CHAPTER 2: LETTING GO OF WORRY

"Our fatigue is often caused not by work, but by worry, frustration and resentment."

– *Dale Carnegie*

**Artist:** Bob Marley
**Album:** Exodus - 1977
**Song:** "Three Little Birds"

O N A SCALE OF 1–10, what is your current level of worry?

For educators the answer is often greater than 10. Being an educator and feeling overwhelmed, stressed out, or anxious go hand in hand. If your answer is closer to 10 than it is to 1, you are not alone.

According to a 2021 CDC Foundation report:

- 27 percent of educators have symptoms consistent with clinical depression

- 37 percent have symptoms consistent with generalized anxiety

- 53 percent say they are thinking of leaving the profession

In a study released by the RAND Corporation the same year, it was revealed that approximately a third of educators stated they work fifty-six hours or more a week. In a small survey my company conducted in which I asked around a hundred educators what emotion they felt the most over the past two weeks, the leading emotions were "anxious" or "worried."

Before we go any further, I want to take a moment to say **THANK YOU**. Thank you for everything you do for your students. I know you became an educator because you care. You love your students, want them to succeed, and want to support their needs. But the simple fact is, love isn't enough. When you pour from an empty cup, nothing comes out. When you give everything you have to your students, you leave nothing for yourself, and you are headed straight toward burnout.

To care for your students, you need to be taken care of, which is why I'm here. In this chapter, we'll cover strategies for spending your time and energy efficiently, productively, and peacefully.

Speaking of peace, you likely haven't had much since early 2020. Saying the Covid-19 pandemic had a significant impact on the mental health of teachers and of K-12 students is no revelation, but it is a proven fact.

Because of these mental health impacts, many school districts have been emphasizing the need for self-care, which is defined as "the practice of taking action to preserve or improve one's own health," according to Oxford Languages. But self-care is often made out to be simpler than it actually is. It requires time and space, and it can't always reverse the damage done after you reach a breaking point.

You wouldn't put down a yoga mat on the floor of a house that's on fire. You'd put the fire out, right? So let's put on our Smokey the Bear ranger hat together and put out that fire instead of looking for a place to hibernate for the next six months.

"Grant me the serenity to accept the things I cannot change, the courage to change the things I can, and the wisdom to know the difference."

Are you familiar with Reinhold Niebuhr's "Serenity Prayer"? The prayer, a slightly edited version of which is shown above, helps you focus on what you can control and change, and let go of what you cannot control or change. So let's talk about the things you can change.

Your plate is full, and some items have to stay there. Putting out the fire will happen when you can remove unnecessary items from your plate, or at least rearrange it in a way that better suits your mental wellness. You don't have control over how many students are in your class, but you may have control over how you structure your lessons and grade assignments. You might not have any say in how many preparations you're teaching this year, but could you turn down a committee assignment or other extracurricular activities? Focus on what you can control to let go of things you can't control.

## ACTIVITY 2.1: WHAT CAN YOU CONTROL?

Consider the things in your day-to-day life that have had you feeling stressed or worried lately. In the boxes below, sort those things into a list of what you CAN control and a list of what you CANNOT control.

| I can control... | I cannot control... |
| --- | --- |
|  |  |

*Focusing on what you can control allows you to let go of things you can't control.*

When we worry about things that are beyond our control, we waste valuable time and energy. I know telling you "don't worry" isn't very helpful, but at least stop and think, "Am I worrying about something I can change?" If the answer is no, I will help you try to focus your energies elsewhere. I hope this activity helped find some areas in your day-to-day life that you can let go of, do differently, or delegate. Let's clear that plate so you can focus on what's supposed to be there.

When worry strikes, ask yourself, "Am I problem-solving or ruminating?" If you don't believe anything productive can come from the thoughts going through your mind, it's time to let them go.

David Allen has a program called Getting Things Done. He outlines five steps for getting things done.

1. **Capture:** Collect what has your attention.

2. **Clarify:** Process what that means.

3. **Organize:** Put it where it belongs.

4. **Reflect:** Review frequently.

5. **Engage:** Simply do.

The Capture step can be modified to help you let go of a worry that you're struggling with. The next time you're having trouble letting go of a thought that is unproductive, I want you to try an experiment.

## ACTIVITY 2.2: WORRY TIME

- Block off 15 minutes of "worry time" on your calendar every day for one week.

- Every day at your scheduled time, set a timer for 15 minutes.

- Say to yourself, **"This is my time to worry. I won't spend time on these thoughts outside of these 15 minutes."**

- Write down a "brain dump" of all your worries.

- Use up the entire 15 minutes, even if it means repeating yourself.

- When you are finished, tell yourself, "My worry time for today is over. I will have more worry time tomorrow."

- If you find yourself unable to let go of the worrisome thoughts, wad up the paper and throw it away.

In fact, give it a try now or schedule worry time for tomorrow morning if it's getting late. Take the full time to worry on paper, in your head, or on your device.

Go ahead and worry now.

_____

_____

_____

_____

_____

_____

_____

_____

_____

_____

_____

_____

_____

_____

_____

_____

_____

_____

_____

_____

_____

How did that feel?

The important thing to remember about scheduled worry time is to let go of the worry when your time is up. If you need more than fifteen minutes, or less, you can adjust over time. Just make sure to give yourself enough time to get everything out of your brain about the worry so that after you're done, you can wad up the paper and throw it away or electronically dispose of the document to get rid of it and move on from that worry. If the worry begins to creep back into your mind, remind yourself that you have another fifteen minutes to worry about it tomorrow.

—

Source:

https://www.rand.org/pubs/research_reports/RRA1121-2.html

Source: Mental Health Impact of the COVID-19 Pandemic
on Teachers and Parents of K-12 Students

Getting Things Done–Keynote In Milan, Part One; Episode 29

The 5 Steps of the Getting Things Done Method

Productivity Made Simple: Where to Start with GTD

# CHAPTER 3: HOW TO MAKE THE MOST OF YOUR TIME

"Most of us spend too much time on what is urgent and not enough time on what is important."

– *Stephen Covey*

**Artist:** Chicago
**Album:** The Chicago Transit Authority - 1969
**Song:** "Does Anybody Really Know What Time It Is?"

**"I** DON'T HAVE ENOUGH TIME TO get everything done."

Does this sound familiar?

"I don't have enough time to get everything done," is the number one thing I've been hearing from educators—over the last year or two especially. You have had more things added to your plate with less help, resources, and patience from administrators and parents. You're being forced to be more and more creative and strategic about how you spend your time to accomplish the critical parts of your job. In this chapter, we'll cover strategies and tips learned from fellow educators.

You are not alone. And you don't have to do everything by yourself.

Making the most of your time starts with leveraging professional learning communities (PLCs). Over the past twenty years, educators have moved from teaching in isolation to learning in collaboration with their PLCs. These might be other educators in your department or grade level, and they are your go-to people. You are all working toward the same goal and can share the workload. If you aren't already, work with your PLC to determine common learning and assessments. Split up the tasks to create materials and share them with one another. Test new strategies together and use the team to review what you learn to make your lessons more effective.

Check your district's website for resources you can use. If they don't have them, search other districts' websites. Even Pinterest can provide a wealth of resources and keep you from having to create everything yourself. But be careful—it can also be a big time-suck!

Some campuses or districts may offer an instructional coach (IC). ICs train teachers and offer feedback, resources, and modeling to help schools and teachers meet goals. If you have an instructional coach on your campus, utilize them to help create assessments and review data. Your instructional coach can also help you locate resources available to you.

How could a PLC or other resource help you with your workload? Take a few minutes to write down some specific ideas.

## ACTIVITY 3.1: REFLECTION QUESTION

Take a few minutes and think about how you could leverage a PLC to help you with your workload. Write down some specific ideas.

_____

_____

_____

Delegation is a valuable skill, especially for your emotional wellness. There's a saying that 80 percent done by someone else is better than 100 percent done by you. Even if you have to finish up the missing 20 percent, this space cleared off your plate will save you precious time and mental space that you can use elsewhere. There are people in your life who love you and want you to succeed. These people are willing to help. Think about how you can delegate some of the tasks on your plate to someone who can complete them for you, at least at an 80 percent level.

Ideas to help delegate aspects of your work:

- Create a rubric for students to grade their own work and provide evidence that they've mastered a skill

- Allow students to peer-grade assignments

- Assign students class jobs to help with administrative tasks

- Ask for parent volunteers to assist with tasks, such as organizing materials or setting up stations in your room

- Ask a paraprofessional, assistant, or other available staff member to make copies or create bulletin boards

You can also look for help from your at-home support system. One educator told me that her husband helped her fill treat bags for the holidays and string bells for her annual reading of The Polar Express. You might even have a child or two who could earn rewards like screen time or an alliance by organizing or cleaning your classroom, recording grades, and more.

## ACTIVITY 3.2: REFLECTION QUESTION

Take a couple of minutes and write down three tasks that you could delegate right now.

- _____

- _____

- _____

Another way to manage and make the most of your time is to prioritize your tasks. You may have heard of Steven Covey's _The Seven Habits of Highly Effective People_. In his book, he presents the Covey Time Management Matrix as a tool to help prioritize your time and tasks for optimal productivity. The matrix consists of four quadrants to categorize each of your tasks and responsibilities—pretty much every part of your life—based on the urgency of the task and its importance to your goals or what you value.

- Quadrant 1 represents tasks that are urgent and important. These are items that have immediate deadlines and are related to your time-sensitive goals. These are those fires you find yourself putting out all day. Covey compares Quadrant 1 to a pounding surf that keeps knocking you down with problem after problem.

- Quadrant 2 represents the tasks that are not urgent but are important. These are activities that require a little more planning or extra work and are directly related to your goals.

- Quadrant 3 is for activities that are urgent but not important. These are often distractions and can get in the way of accomplishing more important activities.

- Quadrant 4 activities are not urgent or important. These are your lowest priority and might even be removed from your task list. Sometimes we spend time in this Quadrant to escape from the stress and pressure of Quadrant 1.

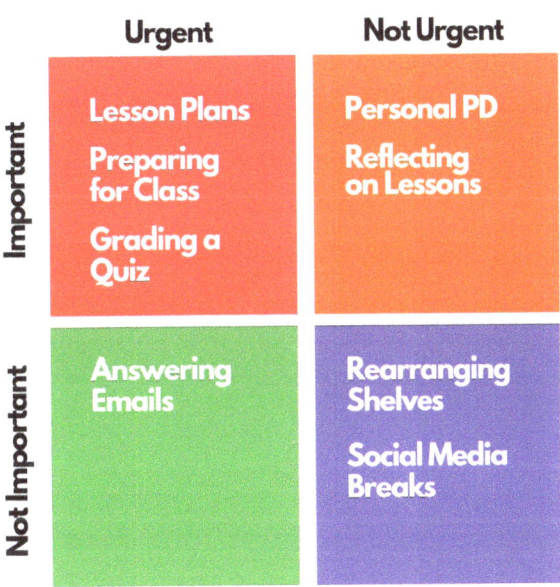

Source:

Covey Time Management Matrix—4 Quadrants (urgency/importance)

Let's look at some examples of where some common educator tasks fall on the matrix.

1. Some urgent and important tasks that may fall under Quadrant 1 are:

    a. Lesson planning

    b. Making copies of essential materials for your next class

   c.  Grading today's quiz so you can get it back to students tomorrow

   d.  Entering final grades for report cards

2. Some Quadrant 2 tasks that are important but not urgent include:

   a.  Personal professional development

   b.  Reflecting on a lesson plan after teaching it

3. The not important but urgent tasks in Quadrant 3 can eat up a lot of your day, such as many of the emails that come through your inbox.

4. Not urgent, not important tasks in Quadrant 4 include things like rearranging your bookshelves or taking a Facebook break.

Take a few minutes now and prioritize your tasks and responsibilities.

## ACTIVITY 3.3: TIME MANAGEMENT

1. List all the tasks on your to-do list for today.

2. Mark an X in the "urgent" column if the task has to be done immediately.

3. Mark an X in the "important" column if NOT doing the task would have serious consequences.

| Tasks | URGENT | IMPORTANT |
|---|---|---|
|  |  |  |
|  |  |  |
|  |  |  |
|  |  |  |
|  |  |  |
|  |  |  |
|  |  |  |
|  |  |  |
|  |  |  |
|  |  |  |

Besides the items in Quadrant 4, those that are not urgent and not important, what other items can you eliminate from your day? What are your biggest time wasters? Do you get bogged down checking social media? Do emails distract you from the task at hand? Do you try to divide your time between tasks and relaxation activities?

Make a list of the things that distract you and try to minimize or even eliminate these. For example, make it a rule that you will not be online or watching television while you are working. Then, when you complete the tasks, reward yourself with a leisure activity.

Take a moment and write down the top three things you do that waste time.

## ACTIVITY 3.4: TIME WASTERS

Think about how you spend a typical day. What are your biggest time wasters? Write down three time wasters and what you can do to eliminate or minimize them in your day-to-day routine.

| Time Waster | How to Eliminate/Minimize |
|---|---|
|  |  |
|  |  |
|  |  |

For more information and a free guide, download the How To Manage Your Time guide from the Franklin Covey website.

Did grading assignments or projects end up in your Quadrant 1? It's something that needs to be done in a timely manner and is very important. Grading can be time-consuming, so let's think about ways to grade smarter!

Ask yourself, does this really need to be graded? Try grading only the assignments that will demonstrate progress toward an achievement of student learning goals. Use rubrics to grade projects and writing assignments. Rubrics help guide students in providing the appropriate evidence of their learning and ensure that your assessment is measuring what you wanted. A well-written rubric allows you to grade quickly and efficiently. And a single-point rubric or checklist is even faster.

Use technology to grade assessments. Create a Google Form and use the auto-grading feature.

You can also create assessments using your district's virtual learning environment or other apps and websites that will auto-grade.

Tips for grading smarter:

- Don't grade EVERYTHING

- Use rubrics

- Use technology

# CHAPTER 4: WHAT IT MEANS TO BE WELL

"Wellness is not a 'medical fix' but a way of living – a lifestyle sensitive and responsive to all the dimensions of body, mind, and spirit, an approach to life we each design to achieve our highest potential for well-being now and forever."

– *Stephen Covey*

**Artist:** Pharrel Williams
**Album:** Happy - 2013
**Song:** "Happy"

F I COULD SEE INSIDE your head right now, what would it look like?

If you're like most educators, I'm guessing it would look busy, chaotic, and maybe even a little messy. Educators are feeling constant pressure from stress, and many are having a hard time making sense of what is going on in their life. Is this true for you?

In this chapter, we'll discuss ways to clear the chaos and make sense of what you're feeling. We will clearly define what it means to be well while helping you take forward steps toward emotional wellness and steps away from burnout.

First, let's talk about the eight dimensions of wellness, which was published by the Substance Abuse and Mental Health Services Administration (SAMHSA).

- **Physical wellness** is about staying healthy: eating well, exercising, getting restful sleep, and taking care of yourself when you get sick.

- **Emotional wellness** is all about how you're feeling and coping with stress.

- **Social wellness** has to do with maintaining relationships and a support network.

- **Financial wellness** relates to managing your finances. We all know that financial stress is one of the most common stressors for us all.

- **Environmental wellness** is about interacting with nature and your environment, be it getting outside or having a healthy indoor environment to work and live in.

- **Spiritual wellness** is about being true to your value system and seeking meaning in your life. It's not necessarily religion; it's what works for you.

- **Vocational wellness** has to do with the satisfaction and fulfillment you get from your career.

- **Intellectual wellness** is about expanding your knowledge and stimulating your brain.

These eight dimensions are interconnected. Each has an impact on your emotional wellness, meaning that everyone plays a role in your overall well-being. For example, if you're not getting enough sleep, you're going to feel run-down, and will likely be stressed out. If you aren't eating well, whether undereating, overeating, or eating too much of the wrong foods, the impact will reach outside of your physical wellness and into your emotional wellness, social wellness, and more.

To summarize, a full cup requires taking care of yourself in all eight dimensions.

Take a few moments to complete the 8 Dimensions of Wellness Self-Assessment.

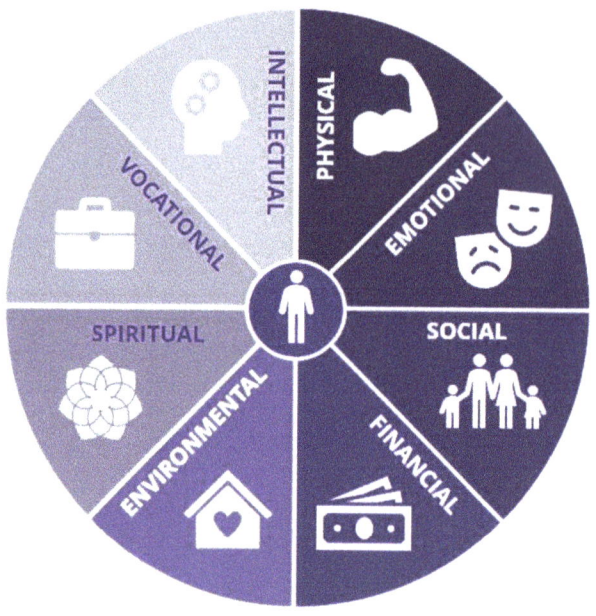

## ACTIVITY 4.1: THE 8 DIMENSIONS OF WELLNESS

Rate each statement honestly, and then list specific things you can do to improve your wellness for each dimension.

| PHYSICAL WELLNESS | Rarely | Sometimes | Usually |
|---|---|---|---|
| I eat healthy meals | | | |
| I participate in a vigorous activity or exercise that raises my heart rate for more than 10 minutes | | | |
| I sleep well for seven or more hours per night and wake feeling rested | | | |
| I feel healthy and physically well | | | |

To improve my physical wellness, I will...

_____

_____

_____

_____

_____

MIKE VENY

| EMOTIONAL WELLNESS | Rarely | Sometimes | Usually |
|---|---|---|---|
| I feel calm and in control at work | | | |
| I feel calm and in control at home | | | |
| I experience joy | | | |

To improve my emotional wellness, I will...

_____

_____

_____

_____

_____

_____

_____

| SOCIAL WELLNESS | Rarely | Sometimes | Usually |
|---|---|---|---|
| I feel like I can rely on a support system at school | | | |
| I advocate for myself and my needs at school | | | |
| I feel like I can rely on a support system in my home and personal life | | | |
| I advocate for myself and my needs at home | | | |

To improve my social wellness, I will...

_____

_____

_____

_____

_____

_____

_____

| FINANCIAL WELLNESS | Rarely | Sometimes | Usually |
|---|---|---|---|
| I am able to pay my bills | | | |
| I put away money into savings | | | |
| My debt is under control | | | |

To improve my financial wellness, I will...

_____

_____

_____

_____

_____

_____

_____

| ENVIRONMENTAL WELLNESS | Rarely | Sometimes | Usually |
|---|---|---|---|
| My work environment is neat, organized, and visually pleasing | | | |
| I feel safe and secure at work | | | |
| My home is neat, organized, and visually pleasing | | | |
| I feel safe and secure at home | | | |

To improve my environmental wellness, I will...

_____

_____

_____

_____

_____

_____

| SPIRITUAL WELLNESS | Rarely | Sometimes | Usually |
|---|---|---|---|
| I live by a set of values that provide me meaning and purpose | | | |
| I participate in spiritual activities (meditation, worship, reading, etc.) | | | |
| I live by a set of values that provide me meaning and purpose | | | |

To improve my spiritual wellness, I will...

_____

_____

_____

_____

_____

_____

_____

| VOCATIONAL WELLNESS | Rarely | Sometimes | Usually |
|---|---|---|---|
| I feel that my job is meaningful and important | | | |
| I feel that my job is financially rewarding | | | |
| I balance work and leisure time | | | |
| I have positive relationships with the people I work with and enjoy being around them | | | |
| I find it easy to manage workplace stress | | | |

To improve my vocational wellness, I will...

_____

_____

_____

_____

_____

| INTELLECTUAL WELLNESS | Rarely | Sometimes | Usually |
|---|---|---|---|
| I love learning new things | | | |
| I read, play brain games, or watch informative TV/movies | | | |
| I participate in creative activities | | | |

To improve my intellectual wellness, I will...

_____

_____

_____

_____

_____

_____

_____

_____

Learn more about addressing the eight dimensions of wellness by downloading SAMHSA's Creating a Healthier Life: A Step-by-Step Guide to Wellness.

No matter how hard you try, imbalance will happen at times. Imbalance may even be necessary. Steven Covey refers to this as Focused Imbalance. Focused Imbalance refers to times in your life when you intentionally go into imbalance for a period of time, like when you have to hustle for a deadline, deal with unforeseen issues, or have change-in-life events like a new baby.

Most imbalance is not necessary and comes from having too much on your plate. When your plate is full, you are likely to lose sleep, have trouble maintaining friendships, and so on. As this happens, your cup empties, and your stress and anxiety begin to increase.

Since some imbalance may be unavoidable, you need to have tools to calm your body down and reduce stress and overwhelm immediately. Here are five tools you can use to calm yourself.

1. **Deep breathing.** Deep breathing has many benefits. It lowers your heart rate and blood pressure, helps manage pain, stimulates the lymphatic system to detoxify the body, improves digestion, and more. By breathing deeply, we reduce the body's experience with worry and anxiety, and we feel calmer. Deep breathing can be done on its own or with other techniques such as meditation and mindfulness.

2. **Meditation.** Meditation is the idea of quieting your mind by focusing on something. Meditation can mean different things for different people, but it doesn't have to be spiritual if you don't want it to be. For those who feel meditation is just for Buddhists or is too New Age, there are also Christian meditation apps out there. No matter what the word means to you, just remember that in meditation, we train the body to adopt a new awareness or perspective of our thoughts—not judging them but simply sitting with them and allowing them to come and go naturally so we can better understand them. A quick five-to-ten-minute meditation may help you lower your heart rate and reduce stress. There are several popular meditation apps to consider, including Calm, Headspace, and Abide.

3. **Mindfulness.** In mindfulness, we focus on staying present. We notice the thoughts, sensations, feelings, sounds, and situations around us. We do this without judgment of how our thoughts might play in the background. We can practice being mindful while doing anything. We simply have to be present with the task or situation we are in. Every time we notice our thoughts taking us somewhere else, we reposition back to the present task or situation at hand.

4. **Gratitude.** A daily gratitude practice retrains our brain to see the good moments in every day, even when we recognize that there are things to be frustrated or upset with. It can be very beneficial to simply write down a few small things every day that you are grateful for. Studies show that this practice seems to lead to increased optimism and improved sense of well-being. Interestingly, participants who did this also exercised more and reported fewer doctor visits than those in the study who recorded negative life events.

   To better understand the impact of gratitude, here's an exercise I do.

   Say, "I am grateful for [fill in the blank] and I appreciate [fill in the blank] because [fill in the blank]."

   For example, I might say, "I am grateful for my cup of coffee, and I appreciate that it's still hot because that's how I like to start my day."

   Now you try it! This won't change reality, but it will make it more manageable, and it just feels good!

5. **Movement.** And finally, let's talk about movement. Moving is a significant way to reduce stress and regulate the body. Taking a daily walk, practicing yoga, having a dance party by yourself in your bathroom—no one's gonna know—any kind of movement is beneficial to both your physical and mental well-being. Studies show that exercise is proven to reduce anxiety, boost immunity, improve body image, reduce PMS, improve sleep, increase sex drive, and strengthen the brain.

There are many free and paid resources available to provide support. Please view the list of resources provided below.

I also talk about meditation, gratitude, and deep breathing on my YouTube channel (https://www.youtube.com/MikeVeny) often, and I would love to have you join me.

**Recommended Reading:**
***How to Meditate: A Guide to Self Discovery*** by Lawrence LeShan and Rick Hanson www.amzn.to/3BoRjqI

***Strength in Stillness: The Power of Transcendental Meditation*** by Bob Roth www.amzn.to/3Uj7oXw

***Making Space: Creating a Home Meditation Practice*** by Thich Nhat Hanh www.amzn.to/3Lm0lcI

***Total Meditation: Practices in Living the Awakened Life*** by Deepak Chopra M.D. www.amzn.to/3zOBE3n

***Breath: The New Science of a Lost Art*** by James Nestor www.amzn.to/3zMuwUR

**Additional Resources:**
Transcendental Meditation® www.tm.org

Mindplace Kasina www.bit.ly/mindplace-kasina

Calm www.calm.com

Headspace www.headspace.com

Tara Brach www.bit.ly/tara-brach-meditation

Jon Kabat-Zinn & Mindfulness www.bit.ly/jon-kabat-zinn-meditation

Resource: https://www.healthline.com/health/diaphragmatic-breathing#steps

**Sources:**
https://homecareassistance.com/e-books/ultimate-guide-self-care/mindful-breathing-can-achieve-tremendous-health-benefits

https://www.urbanbalance.com/benefits-deep-breathing/

# CHAPTER 5: COPING AHEAD

"Preparation doesn't assure victory, it assures confidence."

*– Amit Kalantri*

**Artist:** Bill Conti
**Album:** Rocky – Original Motion Picture Score - 1976
**Song:** "Gonna Fly Now"

THE PANDEMIC HAS PUT PRESSURE on every educator. You have been forced to work extra hours and meet additional demands to support distance learning and hybrid classrooms, and have received additional pressure and feedback from parents and administrators. This is further pushing educators closer to their breaking point, which is understandable and valid.

Have you reached your "breaking point"?

Over the years, I've heard many educators talk about nearing their breaking point, which is defined by Oxford Languages as "the moment of greatest strain at which someone or something gives way." When you "give way," your empty cup forms a hole in it, and you may find you're not functioning as well as you generally do. But when your cup has yet to give way, you can strengthen and refill it with proactive efforts.

I would like to introduce you to coping ahead.

When I was in school, one of my favorite things we ever did was fire drills. The purpose of a fire drill is to prepare for a situation that you hope never comes to fruition. Coping ahead is a fire drill that prepares you for your breaking point, while planning how to prevent it from happening.

Planning to prevent crossing your breaking point starts with paying attention to your feelings. Tune in to how you and your body feel, and the impact of your feelings. For example, you may feel anxious, and the impact of that anxiety may be that you are short-tempered with others.

We often notice the impact of our feelings before we can even identify what we're feeling, like recognizing that we're drinking alcohol excessively before understanding that this is a result of feeling anxious. Going back to the eight dimensions of wellness mentioned in chapter 4, negative feelings can impact every aspect of our lives. Being aware of this can prevent negative outcomes.

Next, identify what it will look like if you're no longer behaving in a way that's consistent with your values. For example, you might start an argument with a person when it's unwarranted. These kinds of situations generally occur because our stress prevents us from caring about our behavior as much as we would normally. This behavior can mean we're nearing our breaking point. It's like seeing smoke beginning to form before the fire alarm sounds.

Finally, identify what it would look like if you were no longer able to cope with stress at all—if you reach your breaking point. What actions would you take, how would you feel, and how would your daily activities change immediately and over time?

By outlining what your breaking point looks like, you can begin to recognize signs that you are getting close. Taking action when you recognize you're nearing your breaking point is called "coping ahead."

Coping ahead is a really helpful way to prevent stress. When we cope ahead, we essentially pre-plan stress or crisis scenarios and prepare for how we can effectively navigate the scenario. When we do this, we imagine ourselves in that stressful situation and plan for ways to regulate our emotions and who will help us. It's similar to how an athlete prepares for game scenarios or how a musician plans out their set and how they will react to different situations.

By the time our breaking point nears, we will already know how we will handle it, and it can be generally less stress-inducing because of that.

So if you are anticipating specific situations at work or in your life that are causing you anxiety or that you think might cause a significant amount of stress, using the cope-ahead method can be really helpful. You could even work it into your schedule by focusing on it during fifteen minutes of planned "worry time."

Here's how to cope ahead in four steps:

1. First, identify what you will need if you ever experience your breaking point. What will help you feel better? What will help you feel more in control? What will it look like to navigate the situation as best you can with the best possible outcomes? Naming these things will help you create a plan. Your plan is like packing an overnight bag just in case. If you need it, you'll be prepared.

2. Second, clearly define the coping skills you will use if you find yourself approaching the breaking point. Will it be taking time off from work? Taking a vacation? Going to counseling or therapy? Going for a run? Calling a friend? Breathing? Meditation? Listening to your favorite music? Identify all the things you'll need beforehand. You'll likely need to use more than one coping skill to calm down or get back to your baseline over time. Committing to relying on the activities that help you will add stability to your plan.

3. Third, identify who can help you. Nobody can navigate emotional stress alone, and you shouldn't feel like you have to. Identify the people who will be safe and supportive to you in the event of a breaking point, and be sure to talk to them beforehand about what you might need. This will help them be prepared for how to best support you.

4. Finally, imagine yourself successfully coping with the additional stress you might experience if you find yourself at this breaking point. Imagining yourself using your coping skills and leaning on supportive people in your life will prepare your mind and body to actually do so if the time comes. Often, just having a plan and imagining yourself being successful using it will prevent you from ever finding yourself at your breaking point. You will feel emotionally stronger and more capable of navigating difficult moments.

Now I'd like to invite you to complete a *cope ahead* plan for any stressful event that you have coming up or anticipate that could happen. Maybe you're fearing a serious conversation with a family member or talking with a school administrator. Create your coping ahead plan.

Yes, you can use coping ahead for nearly any situation, not just nearing your breaking point. You can also return to this plan and create as many plans as you need throughout your life. I suggest building a plan for small situations before building for a serious crisis. Practicing these skills will put you on the path to mastering them.

As an example, I have a person in my life who is a narcissist. Conversations with this person get (very) awkward, so I've created scripts in my phone that I look at before I interact with them to help me shut the conversation down when I need to. I also have specific things I tell myself to help recover from these conversations, and, if needed, I have people I call to remind me those issues are not mine. I have a plan—one with contingencies to protect myself from harmful and negative people.

Coping ahead can change your life and prevent very challenging and difficult situations from developing. I believe in this practice and beg you to try it. If you are having trouble with coping ahead, I want you to email me and tell me what about coping ahead is challenging. Email me at mike@mikeveny.com for help.

Thank you for coping ahead. Your future self will thank you.

## ACTIVITY 5.1: COPE AHEAD PLAN

Answer the following questions:

1. **Identify what you will need if you ever experience a breaking point:**

   What will help you feel better?

   _____

   _____

   What will help you feel more in control?

   _____

   _____

   What will it look like to navigate the situation as best you can with the best possible outcomes?

   _____

   _____

2. **Define the coping skills you will use if you find yourself at the breaking point:**

   Will you need to take time off?

   _____

   _____

   Will you go to counseling or therapy?

   _____

   _____

   Will you use other self-care techniques (e.g., going for a run, calling a friend, breathing, meditation)?

   _____

   _____

3. **Identify the people who will be safe and supportive to you in the event of a breaking point.**

   Be sure to talk to them beforehand about what you might need.

   _____

   _____

4. **Imagine yourself successfully coping with the stress you might experience if you find yourself at this breaking point.**

   Describe what it will feel like.

   _____

   _____

## COMPLAINT CONNECTIONS

When we're going through stressful situations, it can feel good to rant about it with someone else. Is there someone you call to complain to, a text message group you gripe to, or an angry group you follow on Twitter? I get it. Commiserating is enticing, but establishing relationships based on mutual misery is not healthy. When you rant about an experience, you relive that experience and the emotions it produced. While it's okay to let off steam every now and then, be careful about how much time and energy you spend reliving negative experiences.

Social media is not the reason you're stressed out. Every social media site has an unfollow, unfriend, or block button. You are in control of each social media environment you choose to be part of. Be intentional about what you look at, who you follow, and how you spend your time, especially when in stressful situations.

Relating to others based on complaints results in toxic relationships that are difficult to leave. Because of your bond through commiseration, you may justify toxicity. Negative bonding patterns can also include substance abuse and codependency.

Here are some strategies you can use to stop this type of negative bonding:

- Avoid jumping into negative conversations with your peers because it feels good. Once or twice a week might be okay, but if you find yourself ranting or letting off steam multiple times a day, this may lead you to have a more negative outlook.

- Pay attention to the long-term effects in your body. Are the connections you're making with colleagues and friends helping or hurting overall?

- If you really need to let off steam, set boundaries for how long or how often you will have those conversations.

- Ask yourself about solutions. If the conversations you're having only identify struggles without seeking solutions, it's worth asking if you should continue having those conversations.

Take time to brighten someone else's day. Jennifer Gonzalez, who is a former middle school teacher, posted a great story on her blog called "Find Your Marigold: The One Essential Rule for New Teachers." You see, marigolds are considered one of the best companion plants. They help protect other plants from pests and weeds. Planting marigolds next to vegetables will help you grow bigger, healthier vegetables. Find the marigolds in your life! Who are the people who will encourage and support you to make you stronger, healthier, and better? These are healthy connections to seek out. https://www.cultofpedagogy.com/marigolds

- Reduce your responsibilities outside the classroom within reason. Maybe you could make simpler meals, have leftovers, or enlist the help of your significant other, children, or others for meal prep. Remember, it's okay to ask for help. Identify who could help take a few things off your list, and tell them what you need. Receiving help can strengthen bonds in a positive way.

- Forget about perfection. Focusing on being perfect can be toxic. Perfectionism is a spectrum and there is a healthy place for it somewhere in the middle of not caring and being overwhelmed and paralyzed. If you find yourself complaining to friends about your imperfections or if you are having trouble getting started on a task, then you may need to reevaluate your goals and expectations. Learning to say "good enough" will help your mental health and reduce your stress. Take a moment, look in the mirror, and tell yourself, "I am good enough as I am."

- Don't be afraid to say no. Educators are helpers by nature, so it's natural that you want to help people out when they ask. But you have to take care of yourself, and part of that is knowing your limitations. You have permission to say no! Many times we want to say no, but we end up saying yes and then being resentful. Often, we take on too much and then feel like we are failing because we can't keep up with everything we are trying to attend to. It's also okay to say no to the people who want to spend time complaining about their lives. You have to set healthy boundaries for yourself.

If you have trouble saying no, try using this three-step "sandwich approach" from William Ury's book, *The Power of a Positive No.*

1. First, say yes to what your core value is.

2. Second, say no in a calm, neutral way.

3. Third, say yes to offer a positive alternative or gesture of respect.

As an example, let's say the principal approaches you and asks you to sponsor a community service club. You're torn because you don't want to let the principal down, but you also have way too much on your plate this year. Here's what you could say:

"Thank you for offering me that opportunity to help with community service, which is important to me. Because I need to focus on putting my students' needs first, I won't be able to take on a club this year with all my other responsibilities. Once you identify the club sponsor, I'd be happy to provide occasional support to help them when I can."

Coping ahead and reevaluating the basis of your relationships will give you the tools you need to face any difficult situation. By having a plan of action and surrounding yourself with positive connections that strengthen instead of drain you, you can face the challenges of teaching with confidence.

# CHAPTER 6: PRACTICING SELF-CARE

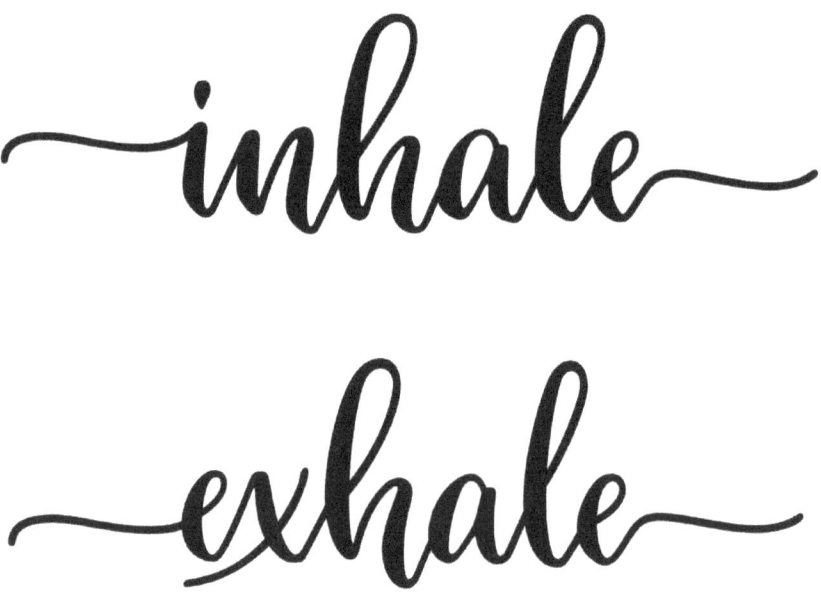

"It's not selfish to love yourself, take care of yourself, and to make your happiness a priority. It's necessary."

– *Mandy Hale*

**Artist:** Justin Timberlake
**Album:** Trolls – Original Motion Picture Soundtrack - 2016
**Song:** "Can't Stop The Feeling"

PUT YOUR TOOL BELT BACK on. After equipping you with the tools needed to cope ahead, it's time to arm you with the ability to take better care of yourself. Yes, I'm talking about self-care.

"If you don't make time for wellness, you will be forced to make time for illness," reads a popular social media meme. It's true. Our bodies can only take so much. Making time for self-care, even just a few minutes a day, can be an effective preventative measure to ward off the causes of burnout, including feelings of stress, overwhelm, and exhaustion.

Before you can practice self-care, you need to understand what it really is and what it isn't. Binging Netflix, scrolling through social media, or shopping may provide temporary relief from stress and anxiety, but are these effective self-care strategies? The answer is no. These temporary stress-reducers can help you regroup and recharge a little, but they don't help you make any real lasting change. These are called escape activities. They're fine to do—but they don't bring enrichment or fulfillment. There's a difference between these escape activities and self-care.

Self-care activities help you take care of your health when you're not in the presence of a medical professional. Brushing your teeth and exercising are forms of self-care.

Let's talk about some examples of self-care activities for your mental, physical, spiritual, and social well-being:

- Mental self-care activities include reading a book, writing in a journal, learning a language, or doing a puzzle.

- Physical activities include doing a workout, practicing yoga, gardening, or dancing like nobody's watching.

- Self-care activities for spiritual well-being include prayer, meditation, self-reflection, and spending time in nature.

- For social well-being, you could talk with your friends, go out to lunch, or participate in a support group.

Take some time now to write down at least five self-care activities you enjoy doing.

# ACTIVITY 6.1: REFLECTION QUESTION

Take some time now to write down some self-care activities you enjoy doing, using the Self-Care Checklist Activity in Appendix 5.

_____

_____

_____

_____

_____

_____

_____

By working self-care activities into your routine, you can prevent burnout and have more bandwidth to enjoy life and work.

Brian Koslow described burnout like this:

"'Burnout' is not a result of being too busy. It is an indication of a lost sense of purpose and a lack of fulfillment. When both purpose and fulfillment are present, you are in a state of wholeness, and burnout cannot exist."

We've all participated in activities or projects where we work for hours on end, but because we love it and we're excited about it, it's not tiring. In fact, we often feel MORE energized by those activities. We've also worked on projects that have sucked the life right out of us. This is a great time to have the "wisdom to know the difference."

When you find yourself going through the motions, I hope you will remember your why and use these strategies for reducing stress and practicing self-care. Having the tools won't change what's going on, but it will make what's going on more manageable.

I encourage you to implement the strategies that feel realistic for you to help you feel better and maintain your emotional wellness.

# PART 2: YOUR STUDENTS

# CHAPTER 7: HOW TO SUPPORT STUDENTS' WELLNESS

"Every child deserves a champion—an adult who will never give up on them, who understands the power of connection and insists that they become the best that they can possibly be."

– *Rita Pierson*

**Artist:** Bill Withers
**Album:** Still Bill - 1972
**Song:** "Lean On Me"

A S AN EDUCATOR AND NATURAL helper, you're invested in your students—not only their learning but also their overall well-being. When they're going through a difficult time and you can't help them, it weighs on you and might even keep you up at night. In short, their wellness affects yours. In this chapter, I'll help you understand how you can support your students' emotional wellness.

As mentioned earlier in this book, when I was ten years old, I attempted to die by suicide. I thought dying was the only way I could escape what I was feeling. I was emotionally unwell. Unfortunately, many students are struggling with the same thoughts, feelings, and emotional issues I had at that age.

With the increase in school violence and since the COVID-19 pandemic began, more and more children are experiencing mental health challenges.

- According to the Association for Children's Mental Health, one in five children have a diagnosable emotional, behavioral, or mental health disorder. Only 40 percent of these students go on to graduate high school.

- One reason for this high dropout rate is that up to 80 percent of children with mental illness go without the mental health care they need.[1]

- Suicide is the third leading cause of death in youth ages ten to twenty-four.[2]

- 90 percent of people with a mental disorder show warning signs during teen years.[3]

As an educator, you're in the perfect position to identify children who are struggling, and to advocate for them.

But wait, I'm not a therapist, Mike!

No, you might not be a therapist, but that doesn't mean you can't talk to students about their mental health and support them. Your role is NOT to provide therapy or diagnose students, and you also shouldn't pry into students' personal lives—although if you're someone they trust, they may confide in you. However, there are things you CAN and SHOULD do as an educator.

- **Cultivate a mentally healthy environment.** This starts with how you show up to school each day—putting your best foot forward, with a good attitude and good energy. It also means listening to your students and providing support as needed.

---

1    Ibid

2    https://cdn-files.nsba.org/s3fs-public/10.%20Schmanke%20Helfrich%20Student%20Mental%20Health.pdf

3    https://www.psychiatry.org/news-room/apa-blogs/apa-blog/2017/08/school-based-mental-health-programs-proving-effective

- **Ask students how they're doing.** One teacher on social media shared that she sends students a one-question survey every week to find out how their week is going. Through that, she's been able to identify students who need extra help—sometimes academically and sometimes emotionally. Some teachers conduct this kind of survey daily.

- **Do whatever you can to prevent bullying and stop it when you see it happening.** Look for opportunities to point out bullying behaviors, including what we call "gateway behaviors" that can also be called passive aggression such as eye rolling, name calling, ignoring people, spying on people, anything like that. Learn to identify them and look for opportunities to teach empathy, kindness, and create connections.

- **Help students regulate their emotions.** This includes modeling the behavior you want to see from them, teaching them self-care strategies, and giving them the space to deal with big emotions when they have them.

- **Identify yourself as an ally.** Let your students know that whatever group they are a part of, they are safe to be themselves with you. It is essential that they know there is no place for hate or prejudice in your classroom.

- **Be completely trustworthy.** Be upfront with them and let them know you will keep things they tell you in confidence unless you are mandated to report something. If you want to share their situation with someone, ask their permission. Remember you may be the only trustworthy individual in their lives.

- **Understand what to look for to quickly identify when students are struggling.** In the next chapter, you will learn about The 3 Outs to keep in mind to notice whether or not a student may be struggling. It's important to memorize this list so you can help connect students with resources that they may need.

Let's take the first bullet point as an example: cultivating a mentally healthy environment in class. How can it be done?

First, expect the best from your students. You may have heard about the Pygmalion Effect[4] (also known as the Rosenthal Effect), which says whatever you expect of people is what you'll get. Now, the Rosenthal study was about academic success. They told certain children that based on their IQ scores they expected them to do really well that year in school. And as you might have guessed, the kids who were told that actually did improve more than their classmates.

What if we apply the Pygmalion Effect to student behavior? When we make negative assumptions, we're setting up ourselves and the students for failure. If you see a kid's name on your roster for the upcoming year and think, "Oh no, I had his brother in class two years ago, and he was

---

4    https://www.duq.edu/about/centers-and-institutes/center-for-teaching-excellence/teaching-and-learning-at-duquesne/pygmalion

a nightmare; what am I in for now?" you're immediately setting negative expectations for that student. You are forecasting failure. Instead, give your students the benefit of the doubt and believe that they will give you their very best and contribute positively to your class and the school community.

Fearing the worst is willing the worst to happen. Every little bump in the road will feel like a disaster and confirm your belief that a student, class, day, week, or activity is going to be terrible. When you expect the best, the best can happen. Start each school year with the idea that it's going to be the best one yet. Start each day with the expectation that it's going to be your best day ever. This expectation will allow you to confirm that your day is going to be great with every positive thing that happens instead of confirming that a day will be terrible and stressful after everything negative happens. You might be surprised by the results.

When you expect the best out of your students, you also leave yourself open to making genuine connections with them. Creating genuine connections, while challenging, is powerful and can promote wellness in your students. Your students need to know that you value them as human beings. Your students need to be able to trust you and feel safe with you, whether you teach remotely, in-person, or hybrid, and there are ways you can connect with your students and get them talking to you. This includes having one-on-one conversations, weekly or daily surveys, a classroom mailbox, etc. The best first step you can take toward forming genuine connections is to let them know you care and that you're listening.

## ACTIVITY 7.1: DOES YOUR CLASSROOM VALUE MENTAL WELLNESS?

Reflect on each statement. Write the number of your answer in each blank.

| PHYSICAL WELLNESS | Rarely (1) | Sometimes (2) | Usually (3) | Always (4) |
|---|---|---|---|---|
| I actively seek ways to make connections with my students. | | | | |
| I ask for input from all students. | | | | |
| I make sure students are recognized for personal and academic achievements. | | | | |
| I know each student well (e.g., hobbies, personal interests, family, and friends). | | | | |
| I empower students to make decisions about their assignment. | | | | |
| I show genuine concern for my students' well-being. | | | | |

| | | | | |
|---|---|---|---|---|
| I set a positive example for students by practicing good mental health practices. | | | | |
| I value the differences in my classes. | | | | |
| My students know I value them as people. | | | | |
| I listen carefully when my students talk to me. | | | | |
| I seek feedback from my students. | | | | |
| I communicate effectively with my students. | | | | |
| I make sure every student is heard. | | | | |
| **TOTALS:** | | | | |

Add up your totals across all columns to see how you did.

Grand Total: _____

- **40–52:** You are clearly a caring teacher who values your students. Keep it up!

- **27–39:** You're definitely making an effort to connect with your students, but there's still room for improvement. Make time to regularly check in with your students and show them you care.

- **<26:** Maybe you are so focused on getting the work done that you aren't making time for connecting with your students. Remember, we're all only human. Make some time to form relationships.

## ACTIVITY 7.2: REFLECTION QUESTION

What are some specific ways you can show that you care about and support your students' mental wellness?

_____

_____

_____

_____

_____

_____

_____

_____

# ACTIVITY 7.3: REFLECTION QUESTION

1. Look back at the ideas you wrote down in Activity 3.2.

2. Choose one action you will start doing this week to support your students' mental wellness.

_____

_____

_____

_____

_____

_____

_____

_____

_____

_____

_____

_____

_____

_____

_____

_____

_____

_____

_____

# CHAPTER 8: HOW TO KNOW WHEN A STUDENT IS STRUGGLING

"The word 'education' comes from the Latin 'educere' = e- (out of) +
-ducere (to draw). Education is not just about putting information in.
We have forgotten that it, in fact, begins in the child's heart."

– *Vince Gowmon*

**Artist:** R.E.M.
**Album:** Automatic for the People - 1992
**Song:** "Everybody Hurts"

ONE OF THE FORMER TEACHERS on my team told me about a student she'll always remember. We'll call her Olivia. Olivia was a bright tenth grader with a sharp sense of humor and quick wit. In this teacher's class, she was focused, did all her work, and had somewhere between an A and B grade average. But outside this teacher's class, she was constantly in trouble.

Olivia lived in a rough neighborhood and grew up in an environment where she was constantly on the defensive. If you were assertive with her, she would be assertive back—she was one of those people. This wasn't "attitude." It was a survival skill in her day-to-day life, and she'd never learned any other approach. There were no conflict management classes in school—although maybe there should have been.

Unfortunately, the school's principal and most of Olivia's teachers used confrontational disciplinary styles that only served to escalate the problems they had with her. If she was a minute late to class and a teacher yelled at her for it, she'd yell right back and get suspended. The teacher on my team got to know Olivia and learned about the difficult things she was going through outside school, and she showed her compassion. This approach helped her be successful in that class. When Olivia graduated two years later, she excitedly and proudly told this teacher—who had left the school by then—and thanked her for believing in her.

The reason I share that story is that, when a student is acting out, this may not be merely a behavior problem that needs disciplinary action. While you can't give every student a free pass to disrupt the class or disrespect you or other students, we should respond with empathy and compassion when people—of any age—are struggling.

If a student throws a chair at a teacher like I did when I was nine, of course there need to be consequences for that dangerous behavior. But we also need to dig a little deeper and ask ourselves, "WHY did Mike throw a chair at a teacher?" Instead of writing him off as a "bad kid," let's find out what's really going on and get to the root of the problem so we can help him. If we help him learn to manage his intense emotions, then maybe when he gets angry, he won't throw chairs in the future. It's a win-win for everyone, and it could change or even save the life of a student.

Not every student throws chairs when something is going on with them. To know when a student is struggling with a mental health challenge, you'll need to watch for what I call The 3 Outs™. Those are OUT of character, OUT of nowhere, and OUT of the group. Let me explain each one.

1. **Out of character** means behavior that is inconsistent over a period of time with someone's personality, disposition, or how they typically behave.

2. **Out of nowhere** means unhealthy behavior that appears or happens suddenly and unexpectedly.

3. **Out of the group** means increased social withdrawal or isolation, both in and out of school.

Now let's look at some examples of each behavior.

Changes in temperament are signs that something's going on—and even more so if it's out of character for the student or happens out of nowhere without a clear and reasonable cause.

Missing school or a new pattern of being late, especially when this is out of character for the student, could indicate problems at home or a feeling of being depressed and unmotivated.

Some changes seem to come out of nowhere. If you notice changes in a student's physical appearance or new issues with personal hygiene, that also might be an indication that they're struggling—or maybe their parents are, depending on the age of the child. Falling asleep in class could also mean something's going on that's interfering with the child's ability to get restful sleep. If a student suddenly stops turning in their work or starts making uncharacteristic mistakes, they might also be struggling with a mental health challenge.

What about the kid who starts sitting all alone in the cafeteria and doesn't join in when other kids are playing? Or the teenager who's usually at the center of their social group but suddenly is walking the halls by themselves? If they're withdrawing and isolating themselves or avoiding social situations, they're pulling themselves out of the group, and this can be a sign that they're dealing with a mental health concern.

So to sum up, you can identify students who are struggling by watching for The 3 Outs: out of character, out of nowhere, or out of the group.

Are you confident that you could spot a student who is in need of immediate help?

There are two steps. The first step is knowing when a student is struggling. The second step is recognizing if they need immediate help that's beyond what you can provide.

Here are some signs to watch for:

- Substance misuse

- Talking about harming themselves or others

- Saying things like, "Nothing matters anymore" or "Everyone would be better off without me"

- Engaging in risk-taking or out-of-control behavior

- Aggressive or violent behavior

- Giving away personal possessions and talking as if they're saying goodbye (even if their mood seems to have taken a turn for the better)

If you identify a student with these behaviors, get advice from your school counselor, school psychologist, or other mental health professional who serves your district. I've provided crisis hotlines and other resources in this book, and I recommend keeping this handy to refer to if a student comes to you for help. **Remember your local mandatory reporter laws.** Even if you are not a mandatory reporter, act as if you are.

## ACTIVITY 8.1: REFLECTION QUESTION

Think of a time you were going through a difficult time in school. If you received support from a teacher or staff member, write what they did that was helpful. If you didn't receive support, write what you wish someone had done for you to help you through that time.

_____

_____

_____

_____

_____

_____

_____

## ACTIVITY 8.2: REFLECTION QUESTION

What can you do to support students displaying The 3 Outs™?

_____

_____

_____

_____

_____

_____

_____

# CHAPTER 9: HOW TO HAVE A MENTAL HEALTH CONVERSATION

"Anything that's human is mentionable, and anything that is mentionable can be more manageable. When we can talk about our feelings, they become less overwhelming, less upsetting, and less scary."

*– Fred Rogers*

**Artist:** Ariana Grande
**Album:** Sweetener - 2018
**Song:** "Breathin"

IN THE PREVIOUS CHAPTER, WE discussed how to support the wellness of students and how to recognize when students are in need of help. What we haven't addressed yet is how to talk with them about this extremely sensitive topic. Here's how!

BEFORE the conversation takes place, you need to take several important steps.

**First**, identify a private place and time to meet. Now, I know that having private conversations is sometimes a challenge in a busy school environment, but privacy is extremely important when discussing mental health. Just be sure you find a place where you can leave the door open.

**Second**, have a plan for what you'll say. Reach out to a mental health professional on your staff or a school counselor who can provide guidance. Don't overlook this critical partner. Special education teachers are also valuable partners when dealing with student mental health concerns.

**Third**, determine whether others need to be involved in the conversation, such as parents or guardians, a special education teacher, a counselor, or an administrator.

**Fourth**, get familiar with laws and policies that apply in your state and district. You may already be familiar with the Individuals with Disabilities Education Act, or IDEA. You'll need to know about other laws and policies that apply where you work, such as mandatory reporting laws and other policies and guidance for working with students. For example, some schools have policies about whether teachers can meet one-on-one with students over Zoom or use text messages to communicate with students.

Another consideration is whether to meet with your student alone or have someone else there. While privacy is important, it's a good idea to leave your door open when meeting with a student, even if your school's policy doesn't require it.

**Finally**, invite the student to have the conversation with you. How you ask them to meet with you can set the tone for the entire conversation. Approach students with empathy, concern, and respect. Be mindful of the environment that you're approaching them in and keep in mind any rules your school has in place for communicating with students.

Now let's talk about what to do during the conversation.

Begin by letting the student know that the conversation is confidential. Advise them of the things you're required to report about, such as abuse or threats of harm. If you'll be sharing the information from the conversation with anyone else, let them know who and why.

Ask the student for permission to discuss the issue. For example, you could say something like, "I'd like to discuss something with you. If you don't want to talk about it, please let me know and we won't discuss it."

Focus on specific behaviors that you have personally witnessed or experienced, rather than relying on secondhand descriptions. You could say, "You don't seem like yourself today. Is everything okay?"

Be authentic and compassionate. Describe the changes you've seen and let them know you care about them. By keeping your statements behavior-based and expressing concern rather than placing blame, you can reduce the student's defensiveness.

If the student ends up sharing something related to mental health, inform them of support that's available. Remember that students with mental health challenges are entitled to a 504 plan or an Individualized Education Program, known as an IEP. An IEP can include a wide variety of supports. Be careful NOT to assume a diagnosis or label; you aren't their therapist.

There is a simple three-step formula for having a conversation with a student who's struggling. Use it as a starting point a*nd then allow your instinct in the moment to guide you.*

### 1. You have to start the conversation.
One of my favorite ways of starting a conversation is with the question, "How can I support you?" After you ask that question, PAUSE and LISTEN. Let the student have the space to answer. Answering a question like that can be really difficult for someone who is struggling. Mental health challenges are generally isolating, confusing, and frustrating. So be prepared for an awkward pause. Another thing you could say is "Help me understand." And then PAUSE and LISTEN. Give them space to answer. If the response is "I don't know" or "I'm fine," remember that it sometimes takes multiple repetitions for someone to feel comfortable opening up to you. Affirm that you will listen if they do want to talk in the future.

### 2. Next, you need to keep the conversation going by asking open-ended questions: Who? What? Where? When? Why? How?
When you ask open-ended questions, you get the student talking. If you ask a yes or no question, you get a one-word response and the conversation doesn't go anywhere. One of my favorite open-ended questions to ask is, "What kind of flexibility do you need from me?" This is a great way to find out how you can support the other person without prying into their personal life or mental health challenge. And remember, after you ask your open-ended question, PAUSE and LISTEN to give them space to respond.

### 3. Finally, don't give advice to someone who is struggling.
As a dear friend and mentor reminded me, when we decide to give advice to someone in a conversation, we're making it about us, not them. Telling someone to "cheer up" or saying "everybody has bad days" will not be helpful to someone who is struggling. Mental health challenges are isolating, confusing, and frustrating. It's important to be sensitive to that. Try to understand it from their perspective, and steer clear of advice or platitudes.

The goal is to have these conversations, which are awkward, to ultimately create a bridge of communication and compassion between you and your student. Let them know you care. Something you can do, especially in a situation where an action needs to be taken on the person's behalf, is ask for their permission. Say, "May I have your permission to share my perspective?" Most of the time, they say yes. And always end the conversation by thanking the student for sharing with you. It's not an easy thing to do and takes trust.

So here are those three strategies again for having mental health conversations with students:

**Number one:** Start the conversation—using "How can I support you?" or "Help me understand."

**Number two:** Keep the conversation going with open-ended questions like "What kind of flexibility do you need from me?"

**Number three:** Avoid giving advice.

At the end of the conversation, thank them for talking about it with you, and restate your commitment to confidentiality and to supporting them in being successful. After the conversation is over, document what you discussed so you can refer back to it later. This is also important to potentially protect yourself and your students in the future. Finally, be sure to follow up on any actionable items immediately.

## ACTIVITY 9.1: RESOURCE LIST

Download this list and keep it somewhere you can access it easily. Consider posting it on a bulletin board.

### Warning Signs & Symptoms of a Mental Health Challenge

www.nami.org/About-Mental-Illness/Warning-Signs-and-Symptoms

### National Suicide Prevention Lifeline

www.suicidepreventionlifeline.org

800-273-TALK (8255)

After July 16, 2022, dial **988** in the US to be connected to the National Suicide Prevention Lifeline

 **Substance Abuse and Mental Health Services Administration (SAMHSA) National Treatment Referral Helpline**

www.samhsa.gov/find-help/national-helpline

800-662-HELP (4357)

 **National Alliance on Mental Illness Helpline**

www.nami.org/help

Text NAMI to 741-741 to connect with a trained crisis counselor

**How to Care for Someone Who May Be Suicidal**

www.edapp.com/course/suicide-caregiving

## ACTIVITY 9.2: REFLECTION QUESTION

Think of your students. Are there any students you might be concerned about? Make a list of any students you need to keep an eye on.

_____

_____

_____

_____

_____

_____

_____

_____

_____

_____

_____

_____

# CHAPTER 10: HOW TO INVOLVE PARENTS OR GUARDIANS IN THE CONVERSATION

"No school can work well for children if parents and teachers do not act in partnership on behalf of the children's best interests."

– Dorothy H. Cohen

**Artist:** DJ Jazzy Jeff & the Fresh Prince
**Album:** Parents Just Don't Understand - 1988
**Song:** "Parents Just Don't Understand"

ACCORDING TO A STUDY PUBLISHED by the American Psychological Association, kids who feel that their parents are involved in their education have fewer mental health problems. This study was specific to middle school students, but it's probably a safe assumption that students of any age do better when their family is supportive of their efforts in school.

Here are some suggestions for communicating with parents or guardians when their children are experiencing mental health challenges.

First, remember that you and the parents or guardians are a team. As a team, you have the child's best interests at heart. Treat kids' families as your teammates.

Mental health conditions are generally isolating, confusing, and frustrating—for families as well as the children experiencing the challenges. Parents may wonder what they did wrong or may be overly sensitive to others thinking the child's challenges are their fault. Be prepared for denial or defensiveness, and approach with empathy and compassion. Avoid saying anything that makes it seem as if you are placing blame. Also, don't be too quick to assume that the child's difficulties are the result of something the parents did or didn't do. You have pieces of information, but you don't have all the information.

Unfortunately, sometimes there may be a problem at home that contributes to a child's mental health challenges. Be sure you understand your legal and ethical obligations to report things like signs of abuse or neglect, threats of physical harm to self or others, and suicidal speech or behavior.

There are young people who are especially susceptible to mental health conditions because of bullying and other kinds of discrimination—including unsupportive parents. It's important to understand that different marginalized groups have experienced trauma that's unique to each group. You may not get it, but you have an opportunity to connect and build trust with people in that group by being empathetic and understanding. Accept and keep an open mind to the fact that their experience is different from yours and different from other students'.

A group I want to talk to you about is students who are LGBTQ. These students are **four to six times** more likely to attempt to die by suicide than other students.[5] A recent survey by the Trevor Project found that 39 percent of LGBTQ youth seriously considered suicide in the past year. More than half of transgender and nonbinary youth have seriously considered suicide.[6] These students need the support of loving, caring adults in their lives, including their educators.

That support can be as simple as using a student's chosen name and pronouns. One study found that transgender youth who could use their chosen name at school, home, work, and with friends experienced 71 percent fewer symptoms of severe depression, compared with peers who could

5    https://www.researchgate.net/profile/Ayodeji-Aranmolate/publication/317582401_Suicide_Risk_Factors_among_LGBTQ_Youth_Review/links/594135220f7e9bd4ee8287d4/Suicide-Risk-Factors-among-LGBTQ-Youth-Review.pdf
6    https://www.thetrevorproject.org/wp-content/uploads/2019/06/The-Trevor-Project-National-Survey-Results-2019.pdf

not. They also reported a 34 percent decrease in thoughts of suicide and a 65 percent decrease in suicide attempts.[7]

No matter where you stand religiously or politically, it's important to understand that using a student's chosen name and pronouns can make the difference between life and death for that student.

Not every student feels safe at home, which is why this subject is part of this chapter. LGBTQ students may come out at school even though they don't feel safe to do so at home. Or they might come out to you, as an adult they trust, but are not yet out to their classmates. It's important to protect students' privacy and respect the trust they have in you. For example, if they share their pronouns with you, ask them if you should use those pronouns in front of their classmates, family, or others.

According to a 2014 study, 90 percent of transgender youth and 70 percent of other LGBTQ youth experiencing homelessness cited family rejection as the reason they left home.[8] Many of these youth were thrown out of their homes by their parents due to their sexual orientation or gender identity; others ran away because they felt rejected or were abused.

These are sobering statistics you'll need to consider if you have a student who comes to you to talk about their LGBTQ identity, before you decide to involve parents or guardians in the conversation. Coming out is a deeply personal decision and is no one else's story to share.

If an LGBTQ student comes out to you, it's because you have demonstrated to them that they're safe with you. That's something you can be proud of, and it's important to continue to earn their trust by treating them with respect and dignity.

In summary, remember that you and the student's grown-ups are a team. However, students have varying levels of support at home. Keep your student's privacy and preferences in mind when speaking to their family, and reiterate to the family that you are there for them and their child.

## ACTIVITY 10.1: REFLECTION QUESTION

If any of your students are displaying any of The 3 Outs™, write out a plan for having a conversation with them.

Time and Place

_____

_____

_____

7     https://news.utexas.edu/2018/03/30/name-use-matters-for-transgender-youths-mental-health/
8     https://williamsinstitute.law.ucla.edu/publications/serving-our-youth-lgbtq/

_____

_____

_____

How will you start the conversation?

_____

_____

_____

_____

_____

_____

_____

How will you keep the conversation going?

_____

_____

_____

_____

_____

_____

_____

How can you offer support?

_____

_____

_____

_____

_____

_____

Schedule a conversation with your school counselor to review your plan.

# ACTIVITY 10.2: REFLECTION QUESTION

Think about a student you're concerned about. Write out a plan for having a conversation with that student's parent or guardian.

Where and when would be the best time to speak with the parent/guardian?

_____

_____

_____

_____

_____

Who else might need to be included in the conversation (e.g., another teacher, counselor, or a coach)?

_____

_____

_____

_____

_____

What do you want to discuss with this parent/guardian? Write an outline.

_____

_____

_____

_____

_____

What challenges might you face when talking to this parent/guardian?

_____

_____

_____

_____

_____

Schedule a conversation with your school counselor to review your plan.

# CHAPTER 11: WHAT IF YOU FEEL YOU'VE "FAILED" A STUDENT

"There is no failure, remember, except in no longer trying.
It is the courage to continue that counts."

– *Chris Bradford*

**Artist:** David Bowie
**Album:** Heroes - 1977
**Song:** "Heroes"

D EVOTING TIME AND EFFORT TO support the mental well-being of a student can feel risky.

Why?

Because we are scared of what will happen if we "fail."

We'll start this short chapter by asking the difficult question that is likely sitting in the back of your mind. What happens if you attempt to help a student, and you later discover that the student has been accused of a serious crime, or worse, died by suicide? If this nightmare happens, you will likely ask yourself a series of questions:

Did I do enough?

What should I have done differently?

Did I cause this to happen?

If something beyond your control like this happens, here are three things to keep in mind:

**You can't make someone else's choices.** This can be difficult to accept, especially when you really care about a person. You see them making regrettable decisions, but despite how hard you try to influence them, you can't make their decisions for them. A student's choice is not your fault.

There are many factors that go into a person's decisions. No matter how beneficial you have been to someone's life, you are only one part of it. Feeling like you should've done more is normal, and so is obsessing over what you could have done differently. But we can't control other people. You undoubtedly had a positive impact on their life, despite the choice they made.

**The results of our efforts may not be visible to us.** As human beings, we want to see instant results. If you go to the gym, it can be discouraging to see the number on the scale stay the same week after week. You may begin to feel that all your hard work is for nothing.

However, success is often invisible. There could be changes happening in your body that you just can't see. In the same way, you might not see the results of your efforts as an educator, but that doesn't mean your efforts are in vain.

Let's say you've found out that one of your students whom you tried to help has died by suicide. First, if you need someone to talk to, seek help. Work with a mental health professional to process what happened.

You may feel as though you failed to get through to this student, but you can't know how important your efforts with them were. This student may have shared advice you gave them with someone else before they passed or shared stories about how you helped them. You may have made the time they did have happier and more valuable. You may have prevented them from making a poor choice sooner. The seeds you planted grow in ways you aren't always able to see.

Trust that your efforts are never in vain, even if you can't see the direct results. At the very least, the student likely knew you cared about them, and you made their life richer while you had the chance.

**There are more students in need of help.** While you can't control students' choices, continuing to help them and support their mental health increases the likelihood that your efforts will make a real and lasting impact. If one student can't accept your help, the next might. Don't let a negative experience prevent you from making the positive impact you set out to make.

A former gymnastics coach, who is part of my company, shared this story, which she gave me permission to share.

"I was a gymnastics coach at a gym. Years after I left that gym, I ran into one of my old students. She was a grown woman now and was struggling with substance misuse. She said that all the years I had worked with her, gymnastics and my coaching were keeping her mentally well. After I left the gym, she quit gymnastics. Since this time, she has struggled with addiction.

While this sounds like a nightmare, it was a blessing to learn that I had such a positive impact on her life. She told me the strength and determination she gained from our time working together was what kept her alive."

Whenever you feel like you've failed one of your students, revisit this page, and remind yourself to **KEEP TRYING!** You influence your students, even in situations where you can't see it. What's important is to put in the effort. You never know what lives you can change for the better, but without trying, you can be assured that you will miss opportunities to help. The work you do is more important than you will ever know.

## ACTIVITY 11.1: REFLECTION QUESTION

1. Think about someone who influenced your life in a positive way. Maybe they gave you some advice you always remember, or they helped you at a difficult time, or they made an impression on you in some other way.

   _____

   _____

   _____

2. Write that person a note thanking them for what they did or said (even if you can't deliver the note to them). Explain the impact it had on your life.

_____

_____

_____

_____

_____

_____

3. Remember that you may never receive a note like this from the students you help, but your influence matters just the same!

_____

_____

_____

_____

_____

_____

# CONCLUSION

Y<small>OU AND</small> I <small>MIGHT NOT</small> know each other personally, but I know that we have at least one thing in common. We both want to make the world a better place. If I didn't, I wouldn't have written this book, and if you didn't, you wouldn't have become a teacher. To make the impact we want, we need full cups.

Educators changed and quite possibly saved my life. Without having teachers who appeared to be teaching with a full cup, I don't know if I would be here today to write this book. You have the power to impact your students on this level, and I believe in you.

I hope you take the concept of having a full cup with you, regardless of where your life leads you. Whether your goal is to be the best teacher, parent, partner, CEO, politician, or individual, the fuller your cup, the more impactful your efforts will be.

You might be thinking, "But Mike, I don't think I'll ever have a full cup." It's okay to be skeptical, and getting your hopes up only to have them dashed again and again can take a toll on your emotional wellness. So does that mean you should just give up? The answer is no.

Are you familiar with the Stockdale Paradox? The Stockdale Paradox refers to maintaining unwavering faith that you can and will prevail in the end regardless of the difficulties of the challenges you face. However, the Stockdale Paradox also maintains that at the same time you maintain unwavering faith, you also have the discipline to confront the most brutal facts of your current reality.

When your cup is empty, it's okay to admit it. You might be tired, stressed, angry, and on the verge of giving up. But if you maintain your faith that you can prevail while understanding your current reality, then I don't believe there's anything you can't overcome.

Not long ago, I went to Starbucks to get a cup of coffee. So that I wouldn't spill on my dress pants, which happens often, I asked for a stopper. The little green piece of plastic is the only thing between me and a terrible day, but I have faith in its ability to perform the one job it was created to do. As I turned the corner to leave Starbucks, I saw a man darting for the door. I moved to the side quickly to avoid him. As I looked down, I bet you can guess what I saw. There was foam and coffee on my pants and the defeated green stopper lying on the ground.

So why did I spill the coffee? Was it the green stopper's fault? Was it the fault of the guy who was rushing carelessly for the Starbucks door to get his coffee fix for the day?

I spilled the coffee because there was coffee in my cup. Whatever is in your cup is what will spill out when life inevitably comes at you (and it's coming).

So what is in your cup? What's going to spill out when life bumps into you? Is it joy, gratitude, peace, and humility? Or is it anger, bitterness, and harsh words?

As you're working to fill your cup, let's make sure to fill it with kindness, forgiveness, joy, words of affirmation, and more.

As a musician by trade, a lot of my cup-filling activities involve playing and listening to music. When my cup gets bumped, I turn back to music to help refill it. I play my drums or call a friend and discuss my favorite funk albums and groups of all time (Parliament Funkadelic & George Clinton are a couple of my favorites).

As we end this small journey together, I want to help fill your cup with gratitude. I want to thank you from the bottom of my heart. Thank you for putting in the time and effort to read this book, thank you for being open to what I have to say, thank you for your trust in me, and most importantly, thank you for being proactive in taking care of yourself and filling your cup.

This book is ending, and it's time to take action. What is the next action step you're going to take to fill your cup? Email me now at mike@mikeveny.com.

# APPENDIX 1: MENTAL HEALTH
# HOTLINES & WEBSITES

The following is a list of resources that could help you to either get the help you need or the information you are looking for. However, I have not personally used every one of these resources and am not personally endorsing any of them. It's up to you to determine if they can benefit you, but if you are struggling, I urge you to reach out to one of these resources.

## CRISIS / SUICIDE PREVENTION

### The National Suicide Prevention Lifeline

The National Suicide Prevention Lifeline is a free service that can be used by anyone who is experiencing suicidal thoughts, family members who are concerned about a loved one, and professionals who are looking for additional resources. You can speak with someone over the phone and they can put you in contact with a local center. This is available 24/7 so someone will be there whenever you need them.

Phone: 1-800-273-TALK (8255)
Website: http://suicidepreventionlifeline.org

### The American Foundation for Suicide Prevention

The American Foundation for Suicide Prevention works to fund scientific research and raise awareness for those who are struggling with or affected by suicide. They provide resources for support groups and professionals as well as to individuals struggling with suicidal thinking.

Phone: 1-888-333-2377
Website: https://afsp.org

### HopeLine

Hopeline is an organization that's made up of independent volunteers. It's a confidential telephone service for people who are in crisis. Their volunteers are not professional counselors. If they feel that your situation is outside of what they are able to assist with, they will connect you to the appropriate referral.

Phone: 1-877-235-4525 (call or text)
Website: https://www.hopeline-nc.org

### Crisis Text Line

Crisis Text Line is a free hotline that has counselors available 24/7 to help anyone in crisis. If you aren't comfortable talking to someone, texting can be a good option for getting the help you need.

Text the word CONNECT to 741741

## IMALIVE

IMALIVE is an online chat-based resource. It's run by the Kristin Brooks Hope Center. They run programs for high schools and colleges along with having the online crisis chat. If you are experiencing a crisis, have suicidal thoughts, or are dealing with intense emotional pain, the volunteers on their chatline can help.

Website: https://www.imalive.org

# GAMBLING

## National Council on Problem Gambling

The National Council on Problem Gambling offers several ways that those addicted to gambling and their families can get help. They provide literature on treatment and recovery options and the hotline can help you get connected with local resources.

Phone: 1-800-522-4700
Chat: www.ncpagambling.org/chat
Online peer support forum: www.gamtalk.org
Website: https://www.ncpagambling.org

# GRIEF

## Compassionate Friends

Compassionate Friends provides help for family members after the death of a child. They offer support through local chapters and online communities. There is a wealth of knowledge on their website and you can request a Bereavement Packet that can be customized to your situation. Through their website, you can find the closest chapter to you from their list of over 600 chapters.

Phone: 1-630-990-0010
Website: https://www.compassionatefriends.org

# LGBTQ SUPPORT

## LGBT National Hotline

The LGBT National Help Center works to assist people who have questions about gender identity and sexual orientation. They run three hotlines and offer private one-on-one chat online. They can help with issues like coming out, safer sex, school bullying, relationship problems, and family concerns. They also have online chat rooms for youth and teens to help them find a community of acceptance.

Phone: 1-888-843-4564
LGBT National Youth Talkline: 1-800-246-7743
LGBT National Senior Talkline: 1-888-234-7243
Email: help@LGBThotline.org
Website: https://www.glbthotline.org

### National Alliance on Mental Illness (NAMI)

NAMI does not provide counseling, however they do provide information about mental health issues such as symptoms and treatment options. They can also help connect you with support groups. You can reach out to the national office to be connected with your state chapter or you can find out more information on their website.

Phone: 1-800-950-6264
Website: http://www.nami.org

### Anxiety and Depression Association of America (ADAA)

The ADAA provides access to information to help in the prevention and treatment of anxiety and depression. Their website is full of information and they do have an option to find a local therapist.

Phone: 1-240-485-1001
Website: https://adaa.org

### Children and Adults with Attention Deficit Hyperactivity Disorder (CHADD)

CHADD's website has information for professionals, educators, parents, and adults who are living with ADHD. You can reach a specialist on the phone from 1:00 p.m. to 5:00 p.m. EST Monday through Friday.

Phone:1- 800-233-4050
Website: https://chadd.org

### International OCD Foundation

The International OCD Foundation has resources and information to help you learn more about OCD. They can also help connect you with trained professionals within your local area.

Phone: 1-617-973-5801
Website: https://iocdf.org

### Treatment and Research Advancements for Borderline Personality Disorder (TARA)

TARA provides access to researched-based information and help to cope with Borderline Personality Disorder. Whether you are the one struggling or it's one of your loved ones, they can connect you with local resources that offer treatment and support.

Phone: 1-888-482-7227
Website: www.tara4bpd.org

# SUBSTANCE ABUSE

## Substance Abuse and Mental Health Services Administration (SAMHSA)

SAMHSA's mission is to "reduce the impact of substance abuse and mental illness on America's communities". This agency is part of the U.S. Department of Health and Human Services. They provide information that can help you locate treatment options within your area. The office is open Monday through Friday from 8 a.m. to 8 p.m. EST.

Phone: 1-877-SAMHSA7 (1-877-726-4727)
Website: https://www.samhsa.gov

## National Council on Alcoholism and Drug Dependence (NCADD)

NCADD works to connect individuals to the right resources in their community to help them recover from addiction. When you call the number below you will be redirected to a local center based on the zip code you enter.

Phone: 1-800-622-2255
Website: https://www.ncadd.org

# TEEN HEALTH

## Partnership for Drug-Free Kids

This free hotline provides one-on-one help for parents, family members, or caregivers who are looking for help with a child's substance abuse. The phones are answered by trained specialists Monday through Friday from 9 a.m. to midnight EST and Saturday and Sunday from 12:00 p.m. through 5 p.m. EST.

Phone: 1-855-378-4373
Text: 55753
Website: https://drugfree.org (you can also email a specialist from a form on the website)

## Trevor HelpLine

The Trevor Project works to provide suicide intervention and crisis intervention for LGBTQ individuals that are under the age of 25. The hotline is available 24/7, the online chat and text options are available every day from noon through 1 a.m. EST.

Phone: 1-866-488-7386
Text the word START to 678678
Website: https://www.thetrevorproject.org

### Teen Line

Teen Line provides teen-to-teen support from 9:00 p.m. to 1:00 a.m. EST for teenagers who are struggling and want to talk to another teen who knows what they're talking about. They also provide resources, information, and offer message boards.

Phone: 1-800-852-8336
Text the word TEEN to 839863

## VETERANS

### Veterans Crisis Line

The Veterans Crisis Line is there 24/7 to support any veterans, service members, National Guard and the Reserve or their family and friends who are experiencing a crisis. There are qualified responders from the Department of Veterans Affairs that you can contact by calling, texting, or using an online chat.

Phone: 1-800-273-8255
Text: 838255
Chat: connect on their website https://www.veteranscrisisline.net

# APPENDIX 2: HOW TO USE A MENTAL HEALTH HOTLINE

If you or a loved one is struggling with mental health, know that you are not alone. You are not the only person to feel like you do, and there are people who care about you and want to help. If you don't know who to turn to, there are plenty of hotlines that you can call. The people who answer these calls are there because you are important and they want to assist you in getting help.

**If you think there is any chance that you or someone else you know might harm yourself or others, contact 911 immediately.**

But if you simply don't know where to turn to get help for yourself or someone else, or if you don't know if you even should call someone, I urge you to reach out to one of the numbers below.

**Who should call**

Anyone can call a mental health hotline. The people on the other end of the phone are trained to speak to people suffering from mental health challenges, family members who are at a loss of knowing what to do next, and people who just have questions in general.

Do not feel that your situation is not "bad enough" or a "big enough deal" to warrant calling a hotline. These hotlines are here to serve people whether you have a simple question or need to find professional help.

**What to expect from your call**

I know that it can be intimidating and maybe even a little scary to pick up a phone and make the call. But there's no reason to be afraid. While each hotline is slightly different, here is what you can generally expect from the experience.

- When the phone is answered you will hear a recorded message. It may include things like what button to push based on your language.

- The recording will tell you if you're going to be routed to a local center and then you will hold while someone is placed on your call.

- A trained counselor will answer your call. Many hotlines don't require you to provide your name if you aren't comfortable doing so.

- The call is entirely about you and to help you. The counselor may ask you some questions about your situation if you are having a difficult time communicating why you called. They will listen to you. They will also provide resources that will be beneficial based on your situation.

Remember, you are in complete control of the call. The person is simply there to help you. They can be a listening ear, connect you with a mental health professional, or provide you with options of next steps that you could take. The calls are confidential unless you specify that you would like them to share the information or if they believe that you are a danger to yourself or someone else.

# APPENDIX 3: MENTAL HEALTH MYTHS VS. FACTS

There are a lot of myths that surround mental health. These myths are a large part of what builds the stigma that surrounds mental health challenges. Believing these myths is what's behind the actions that people take and the way they treat and think about those with mental health challenges. But that's not all. There are many people struggling with their own mental health who believe these myths. That's part of what keeps them unable to move forward toward recovery.

I encourage you to read through this next section with an open mind. Use the information and links provided to challenge and change the myths that you've been believing:

## MYTH: PEOPLE DIAGNOSED WITH MENTAL HEALTH DISORDERS ARE MORE DANGEROUS.

This myth is commonly found in the media, especially after tragic events like mass shootings. The common belief is that people with mental illness, especially diagnoses such as schizophrenia and bipolar disorder, are more likely to commit a crime.

**Fact:** People diagnosed with mental illness are actually more likely to be the victim of a crime than to commit a crime themselves. When there are tragic events such as mass shootings, people are quick to throw mental health into the conversation. However, the American Mental Health Counselors Association has stated that including incidents with firearms, mental health is behind only 3 to 5 percent of all violent crimes.

**Source for more information:** http://www.mentalhealthamerica.net/positions/violence and http://www.amhca.org

**Tip:** Share your story! If more people who struggle with mental health were willing to share their stories, society would become familiar with the truth about mental health challenges. If you struggle yourself, don't be afraid to share your experience with others. It will help everyone in the end.

## MYTH: PEOPLE WITH MENTAL HEALTH CHALLENGES AREN'T ABLE TO FUNCTION IN SOCIETY.

**Fact:** One in four people will be impacted by a mental health challenge at some point in their life. There are many levels of mental health challenges, from anxiety and depression to schizophrenia and psychosis. The truth is, you are crossing paths and interacting with people every day who are "mentally ill", you just don't realize it. While there are some instances where those struggling with mental health challenges are unable to function in society on their own, that's the exception and not the rule.

**Source for more information:** https://www.who.int/whr/2001/media_centre/press_release/en/

**Tip:** If you are struggling with your mental health to the point that you are struggling to function in your daily life, then you need to seek professional help. There are many forms of treatment for mental health and there's a good chance that finding the right combination of treatment options will help restore your daily life function.

## MYTH: MENTAL HEALTH IS NOT A PROBLEM FOR CHILDREN.

**Fact:** Adults aren't the only ones who experience mental health challenges. One in five children will suffer from challenges with their mental health. This myth is incredibly dangerous to the mental health of children because there are many statistics showing that early detection is a very important part of recovery. The sooner the child is treated, the less likely their chance of developing serious problems with their mental health. However, only a third of children are receiving the treatment they need at this time.

**Source for more information:** http://www.mentalhealthamerica.net/positions/early-identification

**Tip:** If you have a child who seems like they could be struggling, do not delay in taking them to see a professional. If they get the help they need now, it could stop them from experiencing further challenges in the future.

## MYTH: IF SOMEONE WANTS TO STOP STRUGGLING WITH THEIR MENTAL HEALTH, ALL THEY HAVE TO DO IS CHOOSE TO STOP.

**Fact:** Mental health challenges are real health conditions. They can be caused by genetics, brain chemistry, and exposure to environmental stressors prior to birth. Just because you can't physically see what other people are experiencing does not mean it's not real. People are not choosing to have it in their life. For example, someone who is diagnosed with depression can't simply decide that they are going to "feel better" and "be happy". This can be difficult for people to understand if they haven't experienced it themselves.

**Source for more information:** http://www.mentalhealthamerica.net/recognizing-warning-signs and https://www.mayoclinic.org/diseases-conditions/mental-illness/symptoms-causes/syc-20374968

**Tip:** If you've never experienced mental health challenges personally, you're doing the right thing by reading this book. Continue to educate yourself on the topic to increase your understanding and don't pass judgment on those who are struggling. Ask them to explain their experience to you.

If you have mental health challenges and are being judged by others, stand up for yourself. Some people won't understand no matter how hard you try to educate them. When that happens you might need to distance yourself from them if they continue to give you a hard time. Talk to a therapist for support.

## MYTH: THERE'S NO REAL RECOVERY FROM MENTAL HEALTH CHALLENGES. ONCE YOU HAVE IT, YOU HAVE TO DEAL WITH IT FOR LIFE.

**Fact:** Mental health challenges are treatable. There are also instances where people only experience symptoms from a mental health challenge for a brief period of time in their life. Just because someone has received a diagnosis does not necessarily mean it's something that they will always deal with. And there are many forms of treatment available to help individuals work toward recovery while improving their quality of life.

**Source for more information:** http://www.mentalhealthamerica.net/recovery-support

**Tip:** If you are struggling with your mental health, don't lose hope. There are many options available for treatment based on the specific challenges you are facing. Make an appointment and get help from a licensed mental health professional. With trial and error, you will be able to discover a treatment plan that works for you.

## MYTH: MEDICATION IS THE ONLY FORM OF TREATMENT.

**Fact:** There are many different options for treatment. Licensed therapists have a vast number of types of therapies that they can use when treating you. There are also options such as support groups, psychiatric service dogs, meditation, self-care, and more. For some people, medication will be a part of the treatment plan that works for them. However, there are some people who will be able to create a treatment plan without the need for a prescription.

**Source for more information:** https://www.psychiatry.org/patients-families/what-is-mental-illness and http://www.mentalhealthamerica.net/types-mental-health-treatments

**Tip:** If you are treating your mental health challenges only with medication, I encourage you to try including other forms of therapy as well. It could allow you to reduce the medication you are taking or eliminate it altogether. However, there is no shame in using medication to help you with your mental health challenges. Find the program that works best for you.

## MYTH: THERE'S NOTHING I CAN DO TO HELP SOMEONE WITH MENTAL HEALTH CHALLENGES.

**Fact:** Many people believe that because they are not professionals, there's nothing they can do to help those with mental health challenges. And it might be true that you can provide them with therapy, but the truth is, that's not what they need from you. Hurting and struggling people need support. They need to know that they aren't being judged and that there are people for them. They may not even reach out to talk to you about it, but just knowing that you are there if they want to can make all the difference.

**Source for more information:** You're holding it in your hands right now.

**Tip:** Look back through this book and pick one actionable thing to do. If you know someone who is struggling, reach out to them. If you don't personally know of anyone, then look for ways to fight the stigma in your community.

# APPENDIX 4: SUGGESTED READING LIST

## THE DEPRESSION CURE: THE 6-STEP PROGRAM TO BEAT DEPRESSION WITHOUT DRUGS

In this book, author Stephen Ilardi shares a six-step program based on his proven Therapeutic Lifestyle Change program. He theorizes that we are seeing such high levels of depression in society today because our bodies were not designed to handle the current way that most of us live. His six steps take you back to the way people used to survive and the way some cultures, like aboriginal groups, still do. This includes the following components:

- Brain Food
- Don't Think, Do
- Antidepressant Exercise
- Let There Be Light
- Get Connected
- Habits of Healthy Sleep

If you are looking for alternative or supplemental treatment ideas for depression, this book is for you.

## THE BODY KEEPS THE SCORE: BRAIN, MIND, AND BODY IN THE HEALING OF TRAUMA

In this book, author Dr. Bessel van der Kolk explains the physical impact that trauma (all forms, like physical, sexual, and emotional abuse) has on our brain.

Dr. van der Kolk explains that trauma can actually rewire the way our brain works. This makes an impact on our levels of control, engagement, trust, and pleasure. He also shares what we can do that will help us undo the damage including mindfulness, yoga, and other therapies.

## ANY BOOKS BY STEPHEN HINSHAW

Stephen Hinshaw has written multiple books that are helpful resources on mental health. He has a long list of accomplishments in the field of mental health, including being a professor of psychology at both UC San Francisco and UC Berkeley and has been recognized by groups across the country.

*ADHD: What Everyone Needs to Know*

*The Mark of Shame: Signs of Mental Illness and Agenda for Change*

*Breaking the Silence: Mental Health Professionals Disclose Their Personal and Family Experiences with Mental Illness*

*The Triple Bind: Saving Our Teenage Girls from Today's Pressures and Conflicting Expectations*

*Origins of the Human Mind*

*The ADHD Explosion: Myths, Medication, Money, and Today's Push for Performance*

*Another Kind of Madness: A Journey Through the Stigma and Hope of Mental Illness*

## ANY BOOKS BY PATRICK CORRIGAN

Patrick Corrigan is a professor of psychology at the Illinois Institute of Technology. He has held many other prestigious positions and has devoted decades to helping patients with psychiatric disabilities and their families. This past decade he has largely focused on addressing the stigma surrounding mental health.

*Challenging the Stigma of Mental Illness: Lessons for Therapists and Advocates* (written with David Roe and Hector W. H. Tsang)

*Don't Call Me Nuts: Coping with the Stigma of Mental Illness* (written with Robert Lundin)

*The Stigma of Disease and Disability: Understanding Causes and Overcoming Injustices*

*Coming Out Proud to Erase the Stigma of Mental Illness: Stories and Essays of Solidarity* (written with Jon E. Larson and Patrick J. Michaels)

*Recovery in Mental Illness: Broadening Our Understanding of Wellness* (written with Ruth O. Ralph)

## I HATE YOU—DON'T LEAVE ME: UNDERSTANDING THE BORDERLINE PERSONALITY

For more than two decades, this book by Jerold Kreisman has been considered the guide to BPD. It dives into the disorder along with its connection to other mental health disorders. There is a revised and updated book on the market. If you are looking to understand your BPD or just want a better understanding of the disorder, this is a great book to check out.

## ANXIETY SUCKS! A TEEN SURVIVAL GUIDE

This book by Natasha Daniels is a great read for teens and adults. It breaks down what anxiety looks and sounds like in our lives, providing practical examples that preteens and teens can relate to and easy-to-follow steps they can take in order to overcome it.

## CHANGE YOUR BRAIN, CHANGE YOUR LIFE: THE BREAKTHROUGH PROGRAM FOR CONQUERING ANXIETY, DEPRESSION, OBSESSIVENESS, ANGER, AND IMPULSIVENESS

In this book, author Daniel Amen goes into detail about how your brain works and what you can do to pinpoint your problems along with what you can do in order to address each area and improve functionality. It includes options like nutrition, medication, and cognitive exercises. If you are easily controlled by your emotions and experience anxiety and depression, this is a good read.

# APPENDIX 5: 13 ESSENTIAL DAILY SELF-CARE PRACTICES

Without a regular self-care regime set out for yourself, you can begin to resent other people who take advantage of you. Your body gets burned-out when it doesn't get enough rest. The longer you go without taking care of yourself the worse it becomes. You'll get into the habit of not taking care of yourself which will make it harder to change.

So, let's make a pact to start making mental health a priority ok? Fortunately, it doesn't take a whole lot of effort to start seeing positive results in your journey. Here are some ideas for ways you can implement self-care practices for mental health into your day.

### 1. Practice Gratitude

When you learn to be thankful for what you already have you won't feel a need to constantly be searching for what fulfills you. You won't need to buy the next new thing that comes out just to temporarily make you feel better.

Set up a time daily to practice gratitude for just a few minutes. This can be by writing down 3 things you're grateful for, or just thinking about all the things you have in your life. This will help you see what's most important in your life.

### 2. Drink More Water

I have a 40-ounce water bottle that I bring with me everywhere. Without it, it's nearly impossible for me to drink enough water throughout the day. I recommend doing something similar to this to make it easier on yourself. That's the thing with developing new habits - they need to be easy to implement. Get a cute water bottle that can carry half the required amount of water you need to drink every day. That way you only have to fill it up twice each day.

Drinking water keeps your body refreshed and energized, and it also helps you digest food better. And when your body is comfortable, your mind is comfortable too.

### 3. Communicate Your Needs

Of all of these self-care practices for mental health, this one needs repeating again and again! Get comfortable with expressing your needs to the people around you. If you need peace and quiet at home for 30 minutes, let the people at home know this. If you need a different workspace than what you have, talk to your boss. Express your needs so you can start working at your best. It's not selfish and it gets rid of built-up anxiety. When you ignore your needs, it can take a toll on your mental health.

### 4. Set Boundaries

I think it's hard to set boundaries sometimes because we don't want to come across as lazy or rude. It's ok to set boundaries and to say no. Especially if you stand strongly behind that no. If you're being asked to do something that cuts into your personal time or that makes you uncomfortable, work on putting your foot down. When you do this, you learn to put yourself first and know what your limits are.

### 5. Spend Time Outside

Always make sure to get outside for at least a few minutes a day. Unless the weather makes it unsafe to be outside. I'm guessing that most days where you live, the weather is calm enough for you to be able to get some sunshine.

Your body needs sunlight and your mind needs this to feel more connected to the things around you. If you have anxiety and don't like going outside, open up a window in your home and sit next to it for a few minutes.

## 6. Stay Organized

Clutter can cause a lot of anxiety and stress. When I let my clean laundry pile up, I get so overwhelmed that I just don't want to ever fold it. Work on staying organized daily. If you have dishes, wash them right away and put them in the dishwasher. If you have dry laundry, get into the habit of folding them right when the buzzer goes off. Staying on top of the things around your house will give you much calmer peace of mind. Being organized allows you to think clearer and to focus on more important things.

## 7. Get a Work-Out In

I know working out consistently isn't easy. And if you struggle with anxiety or depression then you might think it's impossible to work out at all. But, it doesn't have to be. It just starts with doing it for 5 to 10 minutes each day. You can do this in super small sections of time and build up after a while.

## 8. Take Frequent Breaks

Busy isn't always better. It's actually good to get into the habit of taking more breaks throughout the day. It can help to set a reminder on your phone every few hours to get up from your desk and stretch. Even if you are really busy throughout the day, make time for yourself. I know it's not always the easiest thing in the world.

But, everything you're working hard for right now is to have a better quality of life in the future. And one way to do that is by making your mental health a priority so you can be mentally strong enough to push through anything.

## 9. Eat Healthy

Eating "healthy" means different things to different people. I think as long as you are happy with yourself and your body is able to do what it needs to do, that's considered healthy.

If that means eating a piece of chocolate after dinner every night, then do it. Eating healthy isn't always about fruits and veggies. It's about your sanity and what makes you feel good, and finding a balance between that and fueling your body properly. As a form of self-care, try to find the balance between the two. If you had oatmeal with fruit for breakfast and a salad for lunch, indulge a little and have some pasta for dinner.

Treat yourself and enjoy your life, while also being mindful of what you put into your body. Try not to make it super complicated.

Related: The best foods to eat when you're stressed

## 10. Get Some Sleep

Sleep plays a huge role in your mental health. Unfortunately, anxiety can make it impossible to get a good night's rest sometimes. But, if you're struggling in the sleep department I'd suggest making this your number one priority.

Set up a sleep schedule and reduce caffeine before you go to bed. Shut off all electronics and calm your mind down an hour before bedtime. You can even read a book to help distract yourself from your thoughts, as long as it doesn't keep you from going to sleep.

Don't overlook the importance of sleep as **one of the most crucial self-care practices for mental health.**

## 11. Set up a Morning & Night Routine

Morning and night routines can change your life, seriously. I used to wake up and immediately reach for my phone. And would get stressed out when I'd see an email from a client who needed an immediate response. The reality is, that client can wait. And the mornings are your time to enjoy yourself peacefully. You don't have to start the day the moment your eyes open.

And the same thing goes with nighttime. You can wake up an hour earlier and get ready for bed an hour earlier, so you can have time for yourself.

If you don't want to wake up any earlier than you have to, then try to take just 5 minutes each morning to write some things you're grateful for and what you're looking forward to that day.

## 12. Reduce Caffeine

I love coffee more than most people, but I know it can cause anxiety and make you feel shaky throughout the day. It can also make it more difficult to fall asleep. I personally can only have one cup of coffee early in the morning or else it'll take a few hours to fall asleep. Try to restrict your caffeine intake to only in the morning, and maybe 2 cups max. If you're really into caffeine you might gradually want to reduce the number of drinks you have throughout the day. Caffeine withdrawal is no fun and can mess with your mentality too, so take it slow and reduce your intake over time.

## 13. Fulfill Your Needs

Each and every day do at least one thing for yourself. No this isn't selfish and it doesn't make you a bad person. Spend some time alone, order take out, dance along to your favorite music, or watch a guilty pleasure TV show. Fulfill your own needs before anyone else's. And remember, do this often!

## Conclusion

You matter and your mental health matters. It's only when you take care of yourself and fill up your own cup that you can start to take care of others. Just like the flight attendant says on any flight you've ever flown "make sure to put on your mask before your children's."

# APPENDIX 6: 7 THINGS TO DO WHEN YOU'RE STRESSED OR OVERWHELMED

Life is a lot to handle even when you're in the right mindset. And if you're struggling to keep a positive outlook on life then being overwhelmed can be the tipping point.

Whether it's from trying to get good grades in school, doing a good job at work, or just having enough energy to get by every day- being overwhelmed can lead to a lot of other feelings, like anxiety and depression.

You start to easily get down on yourself for not accomplishing enough and it feels like everything around you is crumbling apart. And yet you're overworking yourself and barely have enough time to get a good night's sleep.

Something's gotta give, right? The good news is it's possible to live a hectic life without feeling totally and completely overwhelmed. It just takes some focus and determination on your part.

Finding what really matters to you and let all the other crap go. If you're trying to do a million things at once and only care about a quarter of those things, you'll easily become burned out. It will even make you hate doing the things you actually *enjoy* doing. So, let's talk about some ways you can stop feeling so overwhelmed starting right now.

## WHAT TO DO WHEN YOU'RE FEELING OVERWHELMED & ANXIOUS

### 1. Identify What You Do And Don't Care About

This is what I like to call filtering out your life. Filtering allows you to be more in tune with yourself because you only do the stuff you actually care about and let all the other crap go.

As you look around at your life think about the things you love and want to make time for. Maybe that's your family, your job, hobbies you enjoy, or being around your pets. This is different for everyone so it's important to clear out all the noise around you and truly identify what YOU want. Not what anyone else wants.

Then, go through and identify all the things you're making time for right now that you actually really don't enjoy. Maybe that's going to the gym, being around people who are really negative, or going to college just to please your parents.

If you're doing a lot of stuff you hate doing, you will become burned out. And it's partly from your inner spark going out. You aren't listening to your own wants and needs enough.

### 2. Get Organized

Once you figure out the things you really like to do, then figure out how to add more of that into your life. You get to create the life you want and it's entirely in your hands. You don't have to keep doing things you don't enjoy.

Getting organized helps clear up all the thoughts going on in your head. Use a planner or a calendar to sort out how you will start adding these things into your life. What I like to do is write down a big list of all the things I want to do or have more of, and then I plug those into my planner. That way each week I know what to focus on. And it's a reminder of what's really important. It will help keep you in check of doing the things you want to do and stop doing the things you don't want.

### 3. Make Time for Peace & Quiet

Life is a hectic crazy mess. And a lot of the time we can't control what is thrown at us. What you can control is how you react to it. And trust me, if you're walking around like a volcano about to erupt, you will not be able to control it when you finally explode.

To avoid getting to this point make time for peace and quiet. Make it your intention to unwind every single day. If work makes you stressed out, take time out of your day to be alone in your thoughts. Shut the door to your bedroom, put on some calming music, and put your phone in the other room. Shut out all of the noise from the world. Shut out all of your responsibilities and the things you need to get done. Make time for *you* and make this a priority every single day. It might not feel like it will do anything, but trust me it does.

### 4. Try Out EFT Tapping

I'm not that into "just think positive and your problems will go away" as a complete solution to everything. Because I've tried it enough times to realize it only makes me feel worse instead of better. So, as I recommend EFT tapping don't think I believe it's the end-all-be-all solution. I do believe it is a very helpful tool and a different form of meditation.

I personally can't just sit down and be with my own thoughts, what helps is doing EFT tapping. And how it works is you tap certain pressure points around your body while saying affirmations. There are videos on YouTube with step-by-step instructions on how you can do this. It's simple and fast.

This can help you relieve a lot of built-up tension and anxiety. Coming from someone who overthinks way too much, this is a tool I love to use on a daily basis to realign myself and it works.

### 5. Limit Your Options

If you have an Instagram account you know how easy it is to get sucked into the alternative world. The beautiful photos can make it seem enticing to have a big house, toned abs, or more followers. And if you set those things are your ultimate goals in life, you'll constantly be hustling for more. Seeking more external resources to make you happy. When you can start with what you have right now.

Try to work on making your life simpler, not more complicated. With a simple mindset change, you won't have to feel like you constantly have to hustle your butt off to get all of these things. Start with the things that bring you fulfillment, that don't cost money or require a lot of effort. A simple hike up in the mountains can bring you way more happiness than materialistic things.

When you limit your options, you get rid of all the unnecessary stress you're causing yourself.

## 7. Create an Action List

Start taking action today. Instead of thinking you have to live in this constant state of mind, you can choose to take action. Set aside time every day to focus on your to-do list. Keep taking action every day. Make it a point to focus on the most important things that mean the most to you. You should also focus on reducing the things that don't provide a whole lot of value to you. Put a plan into action to make changes or adjustments to improve other areas of your life. ***Taking action is the best way to get out of your overwhelmed state of mind and move on to better things.***

So if you are feeling overwhelmed, try to work on reducing the things that are causing you stress. Some things are out of our control, and that's what I'm trying to learn myself. Learning how to control what you can and let go of what you can't is tough! If you can ask yourself 'is this out of my control?' and accept the answer, then you're on the right path to making improvements.

## MOVING FORWARD

As you choose to do more things you want to do and enjoy doing, you won't feel so overwhelmed. Learning to set boundaries and stop doing the things you hate will keep you more aligned with your values and goals.

# ACKNOWLEDGEMENTS

"Anything worth doing is worth doing with other people."

*- Tod Bolsinger*

The completion of this project could have not been made possible without the participation, support, and help from a long list of people. I appreciate all of their efforts and am grateful for their contributions.

However, I would like to express sincere appreciation and indebtedness mainly to the following:

Kayleen Holt, Monique Horvath and the team at Scissortail Creative Services, LLC. Thank you for bringing your experience and your hearts to this project.

The team at Mike Veny, Inc., including Cherryl Celeste, Ameerah Palacios, Stephanie Kirby, Laura Kaiser and Christie Stratos.

Laura McKenzie for coming in at the end of this project and making sure that it got DONE! Thank you for sharing your gifts with our team and keeping us organized.

Michael Luchies for going on another wild adventure with me, challenging me and keeping me laughing during our meetings.

And last but not least, I'd like to thank my wife, Denelle, for her unconditional love and support. None of this would have been possible without her at my side.

# AUTHORS NOTE

This book is all about self-care for educators.

So, if you like Fill Your Cup: The Exhausted Educator's Guide to Emotional Wellness, please talk about it! And if you do so online, tag @mikeveny or use the hashtag #FillYourCupBook.

Also, remember that there are many additional resources about mental health that didn't fit in the book. Go to www.mikeveny.com to access videos, courses, live events and special surprises.

## SPECIALIZED CONSULTING FOR YOUR SCHOOL

I also work directly with schools and educators to support them in their professional development. If you're intrigued by the premise of self-care for educators but would like some help implementing it, send me a note at mike@mikeveny.com and I will be in touch immediately.

## FILL YOUR CUP ON STAGE

I also travel the world spreading the message of Fill Your Cup: The Exhausted Educator's Guide to Emotional Wellness and the importance of mental wellness for students. I'd be honored to collaborate with you on a keynote, school assembly, customized workshop, webinar or other professional development opportunity. Just email me at the address above.

# CEU AWARD TRAINING POLICY

Mike Veny, Inc. awards CEUs only for learning events 60 minutes or more in duration, at least 60 minutes of which must be eligible contact minutes. Mike Veny, Inc. does not automatically award CEUs at the conclusion of learning events; attendees and students must earn CEUs by completing requirements publicized in advance of each learning event. This includes Mike Veny, Inc.'s learning event evaluations, completion of post-learning event assessments.

# MAINTAINING LEARNER RECORDS

Mike Veny, Inc. follows strict learner record security guidelines and will only release records to individual learners upon request of the learner.

**The Mike Veny, Inc. Learner Record Privacy and Information Security Policy is listed below:**

All Mike Veny, Inc. learner personal information and training records will be restricted from public access. Mike Veny, Inc. will never share learner contact details with any third party. Mike Veny, Inc. and its partners utilize a standardized and centralized record management system for filing and storing learner personal and training information. This system will assure ease of retrieval, availability and accessibility of the learner training record without sacrificing the confidentiality of the learner training information.

All Mike Veny, Inc. learners can obtain a copy of their learner records by logging into their user accounts at learnstore.Mike Veny, Inc..org. Learners may also request a copy of their record by contacting Mike Veny, Inc. (team@mikeveny.com).

Learners can visit our learning management system's security and privacy compliance page for more information regarding their privacy and security policies.

Learner Records Information Code of Responsibility for Mike Veny, Inc. Learner Representatives

Learner information, including learning event information, which is provided to Mike Veny, Inc. Education Representatives may not be used for any other purpose, or be passed on by the Mike Veny, Inc. Learner Representatives to any other user.

Mike Veny, Inc. Learner Representatives are responsible for the security of all data to which they have access. This involves establishing policies/procedures regarding access security to electronic records, keeping disks or printouts in locked cabinets, periodically updating passwords, and ensuring that terminals are properly signed off when not in use.

Confidential information regarding learners may not be released in any personally identifiable format without permission of the learner.

In compliance with the guidelines in the Mike Veny, Inc. Education Learner Record Privacy and Information Security Policy, Mike Veny, Inc. Learner Representatives will take every precaution to protect the integrity of our student records and any release of academic information identifying a specific learner is prohibited.

### Requesting Mike Veny, Inc. Education Learner Records
Mike Veny, Inc. Education follows strict learner record security guidelines and will only release records to individual learners upon request of the learner. Follow the steps below in order to access your learner records and protect your privacy and records security:

### Requesting your learner records by email
Using the email address listed in your account , please email requests for your learner record to Mike Veny, Inc. or contact us. Be sure to include the following include the following information:

Your Name

Email Address

Physical Address

Organization Affiliation (if any)

A Mike Veny, Inc. team member will respond with the requested record or reply with more information requirements.

**Accessing your learner records online**
Instructions for obtaining a copy of your learner records are here: https://help.accredible.com/logging-in-to-accredible-as-a-recipient

Please email us at team@mikeveny.com for more information about accessing your Mike Veny, Inc. learner records. Please also refer to the Mike Veny, Inc. policy on learner record privacy in the Privacy Policy.

## PRIVACY POLICY

Mike Veny, Inc. maintains detailed records for all learners that attend our learning events. Learner records are confidential and access to the information they contain is restricted to the CEO, Education Director and other team members who have a legitimate reason to review that information.

Learner information will be released only directly to the learner following the learning event and at the learner's request.

## INTELLECTUAL PROPERTY RIGHTS POLICY

Any materials, publications, processes, or related works for the design and delivery of continuing education and training developed by a presenter or outside agency without the assistance of Mike Veny, Inc., shall be owned by such presenter or outside agency. The presenter shall provide Mike Veny, Inc. with a non-exclusive license for the materials under reasonable terms as to use and distribution. The presenter shall grant Mike Veny, Inc. permission to: (1) copy, reproduce, publish and distribute the materials in all print and other formats (including but not limited to online publication via Mike Veny, Inc.'s website, and distribution at future Mike Veny, Inc. programs and conferences); (2) reprint materials for Distribution; and (3) make materials available for purchase and distribution after a continuing Education and training event. The presenter must represent and warrant that the materials do not violate or infringe on any personal or property rights of others, whether common law or statutory and that the materials contain nothing libelous or otherwise contrary to law. Mike Veny, Inc. agrees to provide presenters with appropriate authorship credit as applicable and acknowledgment each time it publishes or republishes the work, and to require authorized sublicenses if any, to also provide appropriate authorship credit and acknowledgments to the instructor's proprietary interest. Mike Veny, Inc. understands and agrees that any grant of rights does not constitute a transfer of copyright and that the presenter remains free to present the materials or revised versions elsewhere.

# PROPRIETARY INTERESTS & REPRESENTATION POLICY

Mike Veny, Inc. will disclose, in advance of any learning event, any instructor's proprietary interest in any product, instrument, device, service, or material to be discussed during the learning event, as well as the source of any third-party compensation related to the presentation. This policy applies to both Mike Veny, Inc. team members and contractors.

Mike Veny, Inc. will reference instructor proprietary interests appropriately in instructional materials it publishes. If no such proprietary/financial interests exist, Mike Veny, Inc. will publish a disclaimer in marketing or instructional materials. Mike Veny, Inc. retains the right to review and approve branding associated with any proprietary interests. Instructor/instructor's employer branding will be limited.

**Trainers do not promote the exclusive use of any commercial product in published instructional materials or during instruction. trainers' discussion of their proprietary interests during instruction is limited to relevant contexts and includes consideration of alternative products or companies that are comparable to the instructor's.**

Immediately upon being assigned to present a learning event, a team member/instructor must disclose any existing proprietary interests relevant to the instructional assignment. Disclosure will be made to the Education Director and CEO. If an instructor acquires a proprietary interest after marketing materials have been produced and distributed for a learning event affected by this policy, the instructor shall provide and document written disclosure to learners at the beginning of the course. Such disclosure shall be documented in the record of the learning event. Examples of appropriate documentation include a written statement distributed with handouts, or a statement included on one of the early slides in a slide presentation. Proprietary content may be used to produce deliverables for Mike Veny, Inc., and Mike Veny, Inc. will make no claim to proprietary interests disclosed in a timely manner.

Prospective instructional contractors must disclose existing proprietary interests relevant to the instructional topics during contract negotiations. The proprietary interests must be listed in the contract prior to contract execution for Mike Veny, Inc. to recognize them. Proprietary content may be used to produce contracted deliverables provided to Mike Veny, Inc., and Mike Veny, Inc. will make no claim to proprietary interests disclosed in the agreement.

No Mike Veny, Inc. instructor, whether team member or contractor, may present or assist in presenting a CEU learning event until all pertinent proprietary interests have been disclosed to Mike Veny, Inc. and learners as provided in this policy. Failure to comply may be considered grounds for disciplinary action in the case of team members, or contractual remedy in the case of contractors.

# ANTI-DISCRIMINATION POLICY

As a company that delivers Diversity & Inclusion products and services it is our duty to be a living example of best practices. The Anti-Discrimination Policy is shared with our team, trainers, clients and stakeholders. It's also publicly available on our website.

Our anti-discrimination policy explains how we prevent discrimination and protect our team, trainers, clients and stakeholders from offensive and harmful behaviors. This policy supports our overall commitment to create a safe and happy workplace for everyone.

Mike Veny, Inc. complies with all anti-discrimination laws, including Title VII of the Civil Rights Act of 1964, Americans with Disabilities Act (ADA) and Age Discrimination in Employment Act (ADEA.) We explicitly prohibit offensive behavior (e.g. derogatory comments towards people of a specific gender or ethnicity.)

## Scope

This policy applies to all team members, trainers, clients and stakeholders.

## Policy Elements

Discrimination is any negative action or attitude directed toward someone because of protected characteristics, like race and gender. Other protected characteristics are:

- Age
- Religion
- Ethnicity / nationality
- Disability / medical history
- Marriage / civil partnership
- Pregnancy / maternity / paternity

- Gender identity / sexual orientation
- Discrimination and harassment
- Our anti-discrimination and anti-harassment policies go hand in hand. We will not tolerate any kind of discrimination that creates a hostile and unpleasant environment for team members or clients.

This is not an exhaustive list, but here are some instances that we consider discrimination:

- Making comments to repeatedly harass, threaten or intimidate someone.
- Comments that publish someone's information as a call for others to harass them. This personal information may include their address, phone number, place of employment, email addresses, usernames, banking details or information about their family members.
- Unsolicited comments that are random or controversial, in order to provoke emotion.

- Comments that contain pornography, sexual language, abusive language.

- Language based on an ethnic or racial background, gender, sexual orientation, religion or disability of a person or a group of people should not be made unless they are essential to the content of a conversation.

- Team members who harass their fellow team members will go through our disciplinary process and we may reprimand, demote or terminate them depending on the severity of their offense.

We recognize that sometimes discrimination is unintentional, as we may all have unconscious biases that could be difficult to identify and overcome. In case we conclude that an employee unconsciously discriminates, we will support them through training and counseling and implement processes that mitigate biases as we indicate in the next section. But if this person shows unwillingness to change their behavior, we may demote or terminate them.

We will not be lenient in cases of assault, sexual harassment or workplace violence, whether physical or psychological. We will terminate employees who behave like this immediately.

**Actions to Prevent Discrimination**

To ensure that our conduct and processes are fair and lawful, we:

- Use inclusive language as much as possible.

- Set formal job-related criteria to hire, promote and reward team members.

- Do our best to accommodate people with disabilities.

- We will also consider additional measures to prevent discrimination, like organizing training on diversity, communication and conflict management to improve collaboration among employees of different backgrounds.

**What to Do in Cases of Discrimination**

If you are the victim of discriminatory behavior (or if you suspect that others are being discriminated against) please talk to the CEO as soon as possible. The CEO is responsible for hearing your claim, investigating the issue and determining punishment.

If you decide to make a claim to a regulatory body, we are committed and bound by law not to retaliate against you.

**How We Address Discrimination Complaints**

The CEO is proactive and responsive about determining whether discrimination occurs. For example, we:

- Look into similar claims about the same person or process to determine if discrimination is systemic.

- Conduct discreet interviews and gather information.

- We will investigate all claims discreetly. We will never disclose who made a complaint to anyone or give out information that may help others identify that person (e.g., which department or role they work in).

We should all strive to prevent and address discrimination. Be aware of your implicit biases and speak up whenever you or your colleagues are discriminated against. If you have any ideas on how we can ensure fairness and equality in our workplace, we are happy to hear them.

# ABOUT THE AUTHOR

"Emotional wellness is the foundation of emotional intelligence
and a core component of Diversity, Equity & Inclusion."

*- Mike Veny*

Mike Veny is fiercely committed to empowering employees to discover the gift of emotional wellness so they can accelerate personal and professional growth. The future of work will require emotionally intelligent leaders to work in conjunction with technology. It's a skill that must be developed in employees. If you are looking for a proven speaker who can transform your attendees through addressing mental health, team building and wellbeing, then you've come to the right place.

Mike Veny is the winner of Corporate LiveWire's 2022 Innovation & Excellence Award for his work as a Certified Corporate Wellness Specialist®. As a PM360 ELITE Award Winner, he was recognized as one of the 100 most influential people in the healthcare industry for his work with patient advocacy. Determined to overcome a lifetime of serious mental health challenges, Mike's career began as a professional drummer and evolved into becoming a change maker in the workplace wellness industry.

In addition to being a world-class keynote speaker, he's a corporate drumming event facilitator for team building, podcast host, and the author of several books, including the best-selling book, Transforming Stigma: How to Become a Mental Wellness Superhero. His expertise and life experience have been featured on ABC, NBC, and CBS news.

As a child, Mike was expelled from several schools, attempted suicide, and spent time in psychiatric hospitals for extended periods of time. His path to eventually becoming a motivational speaker became evident at an early age when he learned how to convince the staff to discharge him.

In the fifth grade, Mike was put in a special education class. Aside from getting more individualized attention from the teacher, he learned that pencil erasers make great sounds when tapped on a desk. He had no idea that drumming would become his path to mental wellness.

As an adult, Mike spent many years facilitating drum workshops for children with disabilities. The project was such a hit that he continued to expand his drumming program, first to adults in recovery and eventually to team building in organizations.

Mike delivers unique learning experiences designed to move past simply educating an audience to provide them with actionable steps they can take to change their lives and work environments. He's delivered presentations to Fortune 500 companies, healthcare providers, and educators, including Microsoft, CVS Health, T-Mobile, Heineken, Salesforce, Keurig Dr. Pepper, and The Wounded Warrior Project. In addition, his reputation as a dynamic speaker provides confidence and peace of mind for meeting planners everywhere.

Mike Veny, Inc. is accredited by the International Association for Continuing Education and Training (IACET). Mike Veny, Inc. complies with the ANSI/IACET Standard, which is recognized internationally as a standard of excellence in instructional practices. As a result of this accreditation, Mike Veny, Inc. is accredited to issue the IACET CEU.

The organization is also recognized by the Society for Human Resources Management (SHRM) to offer Professional Development Credits (PDCs) for SHRM-CP® or SHRM-SCP® and is a Human Resources Certification Institute (HRCI) Accredited Provider.

Mike partners with leaders to customize presentations, including interactive drumming workshops, to fit your event's needs and deliver an epic outcome for your organization. Once you book a keynote, ask about his workshops, books, and courses. If you are looking for a compelling speaker who will connect with, entertain, and engage your audience—all while educating and uniting them around improving wellness—you've come to the right place!

Visit Mike online at www.mikeveny.com.

## CONTINUE YOUR SELF-CARE JOURNEY

## IGNITE MINI COURSE

The world now has heightened awareness around the responsibility that employers have to help employees manage their mental health and emotional wellness. And Human Resource leaders are tasked with the job of figuring out how to make it happen. The IGNITE Mini Course is a simple way to provide your employees with actionable steps they can use to create a self-care routine in their life.

https://bit.ly/mv-selfcare-course

Employee mental health is one of the most talked-about topics among Human Resource leaders. Recent research shows that approximately 40 percent of employees are struggling with their mental health since the pandemic began (Lyra 2020). The Ultimate Guide to Self-Care gives employees actionable steps to help their mental and emotional wellness.

https://bit.ly/mv-selfcare-guide

# THE 30-DAY SELF-CARE PLAN

Are you ready for 4 weeks of outstanding wellness? Refresh, renew and recharge your mental and emotional health with The 30-Day Self-Care Plan.

https://bit.ly/mv-selfcare-plan

# WANT BETTER SUPPORT FROM YOUR SCHOOL ADMINISTRATORS? SHARE THIS FREE MINI-COURSE WITH THEM!
## *SPECIAL FREE GIFT #1 FROM THE AUTHOR*
### FREE MINI-COURSE:
## SUPPORTING THE EMOTIONAL WELL-BEING OF TEACHERS AND STAFF CLEARLY AND SIMPLY EXPLAINED

Since the pandemic, fifty-five percent of educators are thinking of leaving education sooner than planned. Schools are short-staffed and teachers are paying the price. Unfilled job openings have led to more work for the educators who remain.

All of this is leading to burnout. In fact, NINETY PERCENT of teachers say feeling burned out is a serious problem for them. You may not be able to resolve the staffing issues by yourself—this is a systemic problem. But you can address the burnout.

This short course will provide you strategies to support the well-being of your teachers and staff to keep good people working with great students.

In this FREE mini-course, Certified Corporate Wellness Specialist®, Mike Veny will share specific, actionable advice for supporting the emotional well-being of your teachers and staff.

**In this course, you will learn:**

- How teachers are really feeling right now

- Four factors affecting teachers' emotional well-being

- The importance of supporting the emotional well-being of teachers and staff

- Specific, actionable strategies for supporting teachers' emotional wellness

Take this important first step to experience the benefits of supporting your teacher and staff emotional well-being today.

### ENROLL IN THE FREE TRAINING

https://bit.ly/mikeveny-st-course

## SPECIAL FREE GIFT #2 FROM THE AUTHOR
## FREE MINI-COURSE:
## WORKPLACE MENTAL HEALTH TRAINING
## THAT GETS RESULTS!
## CLEARLY AND SIMPLY EXPLAINED

Nearly one in five adults have a mental health challenge, according to the CDC. The events of the past few years are causing many to feel stressed and overwhelmed. These feelings lead to burnout, which leads to higher turnover rates, lower productivity, and increased healthcare costs. And the risk of burnout is at an all-time high.

Burnout was the top concern reported by employees in a recent employee mental health survey. Unfortunately, fewer than a third of managers feel like they're equipped to address their employees' needs when it comes to mental health.

**Investing in workplace mental health training for your organization will:**

- Improve your workplace culture

- Increase employee productivity

- Increase your organization's profitability

- Save your organization money

In this mini-course, Certified Corporate Wellness Specialist®, Mike Veny will discuss how to invest in workplace mental health training that gets results.

**Learn how to:**

- Explain the benefits of mental health training in the workplace

- Explain the importance of mental health training for managers and supervisors

- Describe the different types of workplace mental health training

Take this important first step to experience the benefits of mental health training in the workplace today.

### ENROLL IN THE FREE TRAINING.

https://bit.ly/mikeveny-wmht-course